Four Sublets

For Dande /

Four Sublets

Becoming a Poet in New York

A MEMOIR

Myra Shapiro

Being in your presence is wonderful —
your strength, your smile.
My warmest best wishes,
Myra

CHICORY BLUE PRESS, INC.
GOSHEN CONNECTICUT

June 2012 - IWWG at Yale

Chicory Blue Press, Inc.
Goshen, Connecticut 06756
www.chicorybluepress.com
©2007 Myra Shapiro. All rights reserved.
Printed in the United States of America

Book Designer: Virginia Anstett
Cover Art: Linda Plotkin

I thank the editors of the following periodicals and anthologies in which these poems first appeared:

Ailanthus, "Topless Dancer in a Dressing Room"

The Blue Sofa Review, "French Quarter"

Columbia, "The Knowledge That I Have Everything in the Garden"

Harvard Review, "A Brother"

Jewish Women's Literary Annual, excerpt from *Four Sublets*, "Moving South"

Kalliope, "This Heart"

The Ohio Review, "On an Island"

Pearl, "Marriage, February 15, 1953"

Southern Indiana Review, "The Cadences of Southern Kindness"

You Are Here: New York Streets in Poetry, P&Q Press, "Gloria, I'm Here in Your City"

For their residencies offering me solitude and support as I wrote this book, I want to thank Hedgebrook and the Banff Arts Centre. I am also grateful to Roberta Allen, June Foley, Edite Kroll, Jacob Miller, Eunice Scarfe, HMS, and Sondra Zeidenstein for their good questions and suggestions as I worked on the manuscript.

Library of Congress Cataloging-in-Publication Data

Shapiro, Myra.
 Four sublets : becoming a poet in New York, a memoir / by Myra Shapiro.
   p. cm.
 ISBN-13: 978-1-887344-12-8
 1. Shapiro, Myra. 2. Poets, American – 20th century – Biography. I. Title.

PS3569.H341475Z46 2007
811'.54 – DC22
[B]

2006033979

I wrote this book in gratitude to the Women's Movement.

To Harold
    and the beauty we have created together

Four Sublets

First Sublet

Greenwich Village, 1981

I ARRIVED WITH THE SNOW. The yellow taxi carrying me along narrow Greenwich Village streets made its way slowly. Through the snowflakes I caught sight of an awning, the word *Patisserie*, which I knew faced the only tall building on Perry, my sublet. "It's here, stop," I cried out to the driver.

January, 1981, and my life was about to begin, cold-clear and determined as winter. I was a woman soon to turn fifty, opening the door to a dream, my own place in New York City, my own apartment, albeit for only six months.

Up the elevator, left, then right to the end of the hallway, and there it was, my door, number 3B. I unlocked it and pulled my baggage inside. Leaving everything in the bedroom, I walked into the one other, larger room with its captain's bed for a sofa, the built-in cabinets for paintings and prints, a plank desk, a photograph of the writer Colette on the wall above a round maple table. These were the two rooms of an artist. From the windows I could look out to West 4th Street and Lancianni's Bakery. A kitchen at the end of the foyer, no bigger than a closet, contained on its open shelves expensive cooking pots and a set of yellow dishes.

Without unhooking my duffle coat, I walked in and out of the two rooms, staring, standing at the window, then turned and saw myself in the hall mirror, dirty blonde, curly hair matted from the snow, hazel eyes wide with excitement. And when I finally took off my coat, I discovered the rooms were cold. No heat.

What to do? I went down to the superintendent's apartment on the ground floor to inquire, and there were other tenants gathering, complaining about the rotten landlord, demanding the super call him. To join others in protest, to raise my voice for our rights – this was New York City!

The clogged pipes were a fitting metaphor. I, too, was a radiator insisting on heat. After years of containment, of sitting on myself not to feel brazen among southern men and women, I could hear my voice and it was loud, a warm, weird release of outrage and euphoria. I who love contrast – twoness I call it – had come through snow to bloom.

That first night, leaving my suitcases unpacked, walking out into the snow toward Waverly and Washington Square, the Christmas tree still planted under the arch, the snow still falling, I stepped into a postcard scene, no longer the mother/ wife/ teacher in Tennessee, no longer dependent on books or men to place me.

When I left Chattanooga and entered my sublet, I went through its door as surely as a fetus pushes to be born. Midway in my life I'd come to the moment when I had to give birth to myself, to breach the danger and go forth feet first.

I keep thinking of doors: in Ibsen's *A Doll's House* the door Nora slams as if never to go back, the artist Georgia O'Keefe's statement about moving to her landscape in the southwest, "I saw a house with a door in it and knew it was something I had to have." From the nineteenth century to the twentieth, women had come from books to impress themselves on me with lives I needed to live, opening doors to a freedom I craved. Like them, I wanted to make life fit me; that's how freedom defined itself. And, in the sixties, the Women's Liberation Movement, enabling revelation, taught me to become aware, for the first time in my life, of the way to move beyond literary characters and distant lives to create my own story.

Now I was ready for it, the place that would fit me, New York City. Young child of its ways – I was born in the Bronx – I'd lived in the South from third grade on with the fantasy that only a city would match my energy, and *the* city was New York. Year after year I wanted it.

Three months earlier, October 1980, my husband Harold and I flew from Tennessee to Providence, Rhode Island for a parents' weekend during our younger daughter Judith's first year at college. When Harold went back South to his work, I took the train to spend a few days in New York. Having cut back my schedule as a high school English teacher in order to write, I had some time. And the old longing which always pulled me to New York City.

On Wednesday, matinee day, I was about to get theatre tickets when I decided instead to enact a drama, to be a writer looking for a Manhattan apartment. Perhaps it was the reality of having seen my daughter at college living her own life that prompted me to reject being a spectator. I bought the *Village Voice* and circled sublets in the West Village.

The second place I phoned a woman answered, "It's rented, but the lease isn't signed. If you want to come by in an hour, I'll be here." Recalling it now, that walk along Perry from Seventh Avenue, my heart leaps. If that white building were number 55, the one I was looking for, it would be the building I passed on vacation a few years before, coming from a Sam Shepard play, wishing I were a person living in the vine-covered apartment house on this tree-lined street across from an awning with the word *Patisserie*. And yes, it was number 55!

Linda, the painter subletting her apartment, was to leave in January to spend six months at an artist's colony in Cassis, France. She liked the idea of an older, responsible-looking woman in her apartment, a writer instead of the university student about to take it. In her no-nonsense, New York way, she insisted, "I must know your decision by Friday."

That I lived in Chattanooga, Tennessee and needed to discuss it with a husband was of no concern to her. In two days I had to decide. She had no idea I was playing and the fantasy had turned into life.

Next day, on the plane going home, I ran into a friend in whom I could confide. When I told her what I'd done, the sublet in Greenwich Village I could have, her excitement matched mine. "Take it!"

And when I arrived home from the airport on that October day in 1980, waiting for Harold to come home from work, pacing from bedroom to kitchen to living room through the browns and oranges of our house, the Danish chairs and tables I'd surrounded us with, looking out the window to see him drive up the hill, I said to myself, *See, even the trees are changing.* I kept trying to know what I'd do, what I'd say. I had only two days. I knew it was my dream. But to act on it?!

That night, sharing our news after dinner, I just said it. I told Harold, "I looked at apartments in New York. I've decided to take a sublet in the city in January." There was no saying "Should I?" It was my fantasy, and I was afraid to be talked out of it. He stared, flabbergasted.

As the realization of my desire sank in, this man not given to anger became enraged. His usually calm face flushed. He hit the table, he shouted, "If you do this, don't ever come back!"

I wanted him to understand; I told him he'd had his chance, I needed mine. We'd moved for him to start a business – a success – now it was my turn. I explained I wanted a community of poets for the writing I'd begun to do, that writing had become more important to me than teaching, and I believed it was my true work, the way I wanted to grow old.

Then I compared my being away to that of a traveling salesman. "We can work out weekends, I'll come back, you'll come up."

"*Oh no*," he yelled, "if you do this, don't ever come back." *Betty Friedan*

Only with the words I'd learned in the previous ten years from Betty Friedan and Gloria Steinem and the women with whom I'd gathered in consciousness-raising circles could I know what my mother would never have known to say: "You decide what you need to do, but you cannot tell me what I can do. This is my house as well as yours, and I can return to it when I want." Then I added, "I refuse to say years from now *If only....*" *Gloria Steinem*

"You're abandoning me," he confided as his voice softened. Then it rose, "Don't think I'm ever coming to New York."

He walked out of the dining room. I heard him in the bedroom collecting things he always took out of his pockets to unload on the dresser after the day at work. Coming through the kitchen, holding his car keys, he marched out the door into the driveway. I heard the engine, the car in reverse, the tires screeching. Since he had no close friends, and he never went out by himself once he was home, I didn't know where he'd go or what he'd do.

I was frightened but not hesitant. Suddenly I had to go forward, I had to. It was not about marriage, not about this man or any man. I was about to stop longing, I was about to give birth to a life.

At twenty I'd married; at twenty-three the first of our two children was born. Good student I'd walked lock-step to the conventions of my day. But where was my life? I created a home which didn't often engage me and raised daughters through the stages books told me they were going through. Even now as I write I don't want to dwell there. Not yet. Not until I come to where my life lives. What pulls me now is the desire for where I was going.

The night before I leave Chattanooga to take the apartment in the Village, I can't calm my heart or stomach, nor can I turn to Harold to say anything about it. And when finally I sleep, I have no dreams to give me clues. But on the plane to New York I read a review in the local paper written by a friend at the university about a television production of *Hamlet*. In it are words to sustain me, to lift me, the last lines of the play which, for almost ten years, I'd taught to high school seniors: "For he would have proved, had he been put on, most royal." I feel I am about to be put on, to play the role I was born for.

New York City is the kingdom. I know it's not about ease but possibility. Creativity. There's a woman in the harbor wearing a crown, welcoming those who enter – she stands in an ocean! – with one hand holding a green light, the other a book. That's nobility here, making art in a city lit up with permission, fulfilling promises, GO.

(handwritten margin note: Lady Liberty)

My first days I feel I'm on a movie set: people in my neighborhood look like Greenwich Village parodies: at lunch beside me in a restaurant called Arnold's Turtle, a man who could double for Trotsky holds *Madame Bovary*; at the next table a woman with a blue streak in her gray hair reads *Spoon River Anthology*. These are adults, not young students; nowhere in Chattanooga have I felt the kinship of this scene, the intellect, the color of such characters, and the pleasure of one's privacy in public places.

Outings for groceries hold adventure: I cross the street to a health store as the police arrive to arrest a nice looking young man for passing bad checks. "What will happen to me?" the boy asks the cop. The cop, ignoring him, tells the storeowner, "You're lucky I'm even dealing with this." I sympathize with the shop owner, and I want to laugh at the policeman's chutzpah. I wonder what will happen to the boy. All in five minutes. I pay for my sunflower seeds and leave.

In a liquor store I buy sherry to go with the sunflower seeds. The old man in the store notices the New School catalogue I'm carrying. Somehow he can tell I'm new; he asks and I say I'm from Tennessee, that I'm in New York to write. He doesn't seem to think that's unusual. He tells me he once played trumpet in Chattanooga at the Panorama on Lookout Mountain. A connection established, he welcomes me to his neighborhood and gives me his card. "If you ever need a check cashed, I'll be glad to cash it." I begin to see how the city works, as neighborhoods, each one distinctive, the Village a village!

Of course my euphoria has to be tempered with some grounding. Oohing and ahhing over everything, oblivious of garbage piled up on the curbs, I'm walking back to the sublet from Sheridan Square after browsing in the bookstore on its corner late one night. At the hub of the square, several village streets come together, and, by chance, I start west on Christopher instead of the more direct West 4th Street beside it. It's after midnight yet the streets are full.

I'll get to Perry by turning from Bleecker, and I revel – how entertaining, how charming whatever the direction – as I look in little shop windows at clothes and antiques right next to greengrocers with their pyramids of fruit and flowers. In love with everything.

When I reach Perry I turn right, one block to my apartment. Perry is lit but much quieter; here I'm the only one walking. Except for my building it's a street of old brownstone houses. One car passes. I see it stop as I turn to go into my building.

Something makes me suspicious; immediately I dismiss it – how silly – the car must be backing up because it's lost.

As I unlock the inner lobby door, at the moment it clicks shut, a young, pudgy man in a rumpled, white shirt runs through the front door from the street. The inner door is glass, and he's knocking on it, mouthing the name *Joseph*, indicating he wants in.

I'm polite, I pause, but somehow aware of New York City protocol, I point to the panel of buttons to ring on the outer wall to the left of him, then look toward the elevator as he turns toward the row of bells. But he's at the glass door again, knocking.

As I look at him, his flailing arms raised, I see his pants are open, his penis pulled out, hanging down. Quickly I turn away, the glass wall and the locked door protect me; the elevator is coming. *Please. Please.* Just then two men calmly enter the building, and he's talking to them. They pass him without pausing, without looking down at his unzipped pants! They're pushing a button on the wall – I want to wait to tell them this man should be reported, but the elevator is here, I have it, I enter and leave trouble behind.

My lesson is what? Don't stroll on quiet streets? Always use West 4th Street after midnight? Yes, and don't be stupidly romantic or naive. So, sharpening my senses, developing peripheral vision, I walk into my apartment and turn on the light. Alert to last night's cockroaches, I scan for movement. I've placed boric acid around the room. They don't appear. But I won't get cocky. I just feel lucky to be fighting one fear at a time.

Building muscles I call it. In the freedom of the city is indifference, people busy with their own lives, which forces you to find your own strength. I like the stretch, the energy of that struggle.

I can't stop thinking about the Statue of Liberty, the lady in the harbor not far from the Village. Tomorrow I plan to walk to see her. She was my parents' first green in this new world, my inheritance, and I am aware of how much I, yearning to breathe free, insist on holding to the dream of her.

About four weeks after I'm in the sublet, in February, which is the month of our wedding anniversary, Harold catches the last plane from Chattanooga on a Friday night to arrive at La-Guardia around ten. By the time he gets to the apartment it's eleven. I've been waiting, eager to have him here. He's eating his words, that if I go to New York he will never visit, and I want to make this weekend worth each difficult bite. I've gone back to Tennessee for a long weekend; now, maybe out of curiosity, maybe having taken in my happiness, he's coming. For these two days I will do what I can to help him be happy.

I've planned the hours like a social director on a cruise ship, and I'm starting right off with the Lion's Head at midnight. He'll feel masculine in its pub-like atmosphere, and he'll be comforted by the good, solid food. It will bring the neighborhood to him: electric, friendly, and entertaining.

He's here! He's buzzed from downstairs; I run to the elevator. The door opens and we kiss. Nervous, I have to rescue his suitcase from the door's closing.

"Where should it go?" He wants to know where to put his Hartman carry-on. He wants to know where to put his solid 5'8" roundness. "There's hardly room here for us, much less our belongings," he mumbles.

He's used to a house. The beauty of an artist's two-room apartment – the photograph of Colette leaning near a vase of flowers, the beautiful blue and yellow geometric fabric on the cushions of the maple folding chairs around the circular table just the right scale for the entryway to the living room – does not charm him. He begins to sneeze.

I'm calm; this time I do not absorb his discomfort. He's here, I'm content. "There's a wonderful, cozy bar-restaurant just a few blocks away," I offer. "We could have a light something to eat, a drink maybe, before we call it a night. It's still early." Which is true; we hardly ever go to bed before one.

He doesn't answer, keeps sneezing. So I quietly prepare for bed. Maybe my silence helps him reconsider.

"Yes," he says. "Let's go out, I haven't eaten. But isn't it too late to be served? Too late to be walking on the streets? Is it safe?" he asks, sneezing.

We go out onto softly-lit Perry Street. It's cold so we lock arms, stay close. His bulk warms me. Together we blend, our eyes the same hazel, our hair thick and curly. Pointing to Lancianni's on West 4th where, I tell him, the smell of croissants baking will wake us in the morning, I see him smile. He loves a good breakfast. I show him the little Thai restaurant on 10th Street where I often eat dinner. At Seventh Avenue where cars fill the lanes as if it were noon instead of late night, we cross to Christopher and step down into the Lion's Head which is packed with animated bodies full of loud talk, warm and wonderfully inviting to come into on this February night.

There's a table for us in the crowded room behind the bar. Seated, looking up through the little window the level of the sidewalk, Harold laughs to see peoples' boots go by. A waitress hands us menus and smiles.

"You know, this is where Jessica Lange was discovered waiting tables. By Jack Nicholson I think." I'm telling him this, tickled to share news of such an inside nature. He loves going to movies and theatre; now he can see there are budding stars all around us.

When a bowl of chowder and the Caesar salad come, he purrs "This is delicious" to the steam rising from the bowl. The romaine is crisp, the anchovies plenty. Everything.

About two weeks before I came to New York, my mother's

old friend phoned early one morning. She must have been troubled for days. I was only half awake, but she had to tell me, she *had to*:

"Your mother's not alive so I feel it's my duty to warn you as surely she would have. You're married to a prince. If you go away and leave him here alone, women will line up to invite him for dinner when he comes home from a long day's work; they'll cook, they'll find the way to his heart – they know how – and you'll lose him."

When I said I had to risk that, she upped her ante. "For what it will cost you, the two of you could have everything, travel around the world."

"Molly," I said, "you're right, I love to travel, and it's what I've always done to make life exciting. For years I'd scrimp on food, I'd find bargains to save for trips. But now Harold's built a successful business and we have money. We can afford to be generous with ourselves."

With the last statement I sensed I was losing her. I knew how to reach her. "Molly, the sublet in New York City is my fur coat, my diamond ring after thirty years of marriage." That she understood. "If I don't get this dream, I'll grow old saying *If only*. Living with a shrew won't make him happy."

As I sip my wine, watching this man I'd married when I was twenty, the man whose mother had cooked for hundreds as the wife of a rabbi, this southerner who likes when people smile at him and care to please him and refill his water glass, I see his pleasure in this lovely, simple meal in my neighborhood restaurant, and it feels good.

I've created a family, a history, with a good man. It's as if that were a launching pad, the secure place from which to give rise to my deeper story, one where I take on new family, poets who will touch me where I've never been touched.

Arriving in New York at the start of 1981, in time to enter the winter term of classes, I've been accepted into a workshop at the 92nd Street Y, famous for poetry, where Dylan Thomas sang his poems, and T. S. Eliot mumbled his, where each season famous writers come to give readings and teach classes. These are gods to me, and I am to study in the place where the ancients stood and tradition is nurtured. In order to attend a workshop, I am required to submit poems. I've been accepted!

The New School is just a few blocks from my sublet, and I decide to enroll in a class there as well. That class requires only a fee and showing up. How better to spend an evening than with other writers, with a good teacher and our poems? So it's two workshops, and I'm eager and ready.

Each morning I'm in my sublet, reading and writing, but by mid-afternoon I hit the streets. For a long time I'm unable to let go of the knowledge that I'm not a tourist. I must see everything so everyday I'm out and running. Each night I go to class or an event or meet someone for dinner – theatre, museums, readings, the choices often conflict. I can't believe they're mine to make.

I am thrilled to be here as a writer, a maker in this city of creators, where no one is making a big fuss over my special occupation or my age. I am one of many, and I don't feel threatened by the fact that I'm a beginner. To be a big fish in a small pond is not what I need.

The New School class begins before the Y workshop. Colette Inez, a poet whose work I don't know yet, is the teacher, and on the first evening we're to go around the room of about thirty students to say why we've come. Briefly, I tell my story, that I'm subletting an apartment in the city for the semester, that I'm from Chattanooga, where my husband and I live, that I want to study to become a better writer and need a community of other poets.

When the class is over I am surrounded by women who are struck by what I've said. It surprises me, the importance to them of my having left home to do what I wanted. I feel courageous. Some of us go to the Peacock Cafe where the owners let you sit for hours over one cappuccino.

As I walk back to the apartment, I realize these women I met are in their twenties and thirties, and their admiration may be not only for my coming to New York from Tennessee at my age but also for my passion, that I am determined to become a poet, to find the life that wants to live in me.

Colette Inez seems to enjoy the city as much as I do, and she instructs us to use it, take note as we ride the subway, read signs, eavesdrop on conversations. She is a woman about my age who came to New York from what I sense was a mysterious, difficult life in Europe. She announces she will invite guest poets to our class. What will surprise me is that they will be close to my age, and though they are not beginners, though they are accomplished, their careers as writers began late and are not yet established. They've been published, they work steadily. These poets give me contemporary models. For our next class I bring in my first New York poem:

GLORIA, I'M HERE IN YOUR CITY

Even rain pulls me to the street. Late
Last night I took myself to the Lion's Head
And the city, my street,
West 4th and Perry was gold,
A glaze on wet pavement, brownstone
Windows, stoops, Charlie & Kelly's on the corner.
As if a fresh salad had been prepared,
A glorious blend of garlic, oil and vinegar
And it was being tossed at my table.

I enter the great tradition. The workshop sponsored by the
92nd Street Y Poetry Center is to meet at the apartment of the
teacher, Judith Johnson Sherwin. I take the C train to Central
Park West and find myself in a living room facing so much
beauty I cannot believe it exists daily for someone's eyes: Central Park. Its huge reservoir shimmers, the snow falls softly on
trees under lamplight, and across the stretch of it, the apartment buildings on Fifth Avenue dazzle the night.

A year before coming to New York I dreamed I rode in a
carriage through this park to others waiting at the entrance of
a grand building. Though I was in twentieth century clothes,
everything seemed lit by the past: the combs of another century's jeweled women and the silver-topped canes of top-hatted
men. The roadways glistened with lamplight and fresh rain.
That dream and the poetic tradition will come to meet in Judith
Sherwin's apartment.

When I arrive, Ms. Sherwin comes to the door to welcome
me, looking so comfortable and unassuming in loose pants and
an old shirt, I wonder if it's she, the poet whose four books I
bought when the Y called to say I'd been accepted to her class.

"Judith Sherwin?" I question.

"Just call me Judith," she says, excusing herself to tend to
children in another room. "Make yourself at home; you're the
first one here." And I go to those windows over the Park.

When the other students come, we take seats on an old-
fashioned, dark sofa and big upholstered chairs; side chairs are
pulled from the dining room to form us in a circle.

Judith begins: "When I was in a workshop with Muriel
Rukeyser, she began by having all of us read, listen to, repeat,
then write down Gerard Manley Hopkins' 'Pied Beauty'."

And now we begin: "Glory be...." I raise my eyes to the
lights across the park, dizzy with happiness. I have to force myself to concentrate. Judith Johnson Sherwin, daughter of the
biographer of Charles Dickens, a poet who carries the name I

gave *my* daughter, is teaching me to be a poet as she was taught by Muriel Rukeyser praising Gerard Manley Hopkins. At such a moment no one is dead, my life has passed beyond all time, to even beyond anything I ever dreamed. *Glory be to God*

My mind can't stay focused. Judith is giving us an assign-ment. I'll need to stay after class to ask for instructions. Judith announces, "Next week I'll have a jug of wine. Poets must have wine for the work and the talk to go well." Glory be to God.

Only, I think, by next week what if someone phones from home, some emergency, an illness – the hook, I've come to call it – to pull me back to Chattanooga. This is purer happiness than I have ever known, and I'll just have to live with a mem-ory, that I am lucky beyond measure to have had this much.

Some of us linger in the lobby, making plans to meet, per-haps dinner before the next workshop, or why not walk up to Columbus Avenue now for coffee. We find a diner on the cor-ner of Columbus and 86th Street and talk about the class and each other and the view from that window. We already know things about ourselves from our poems: Patty, whose poem about mayo on a BLT impressed me as sharp and clear and modern, gives me permission to write about the ordinary; Lois, whose poem so lovingly remembered a trip with her father to the Planetarium, suggests the experience of the city as a subject natural as magnolias; Olive, in New York from Texas with a poem immediately kindred in its echo of my domestic life and longing, supports my reality. The woman who looks a bit like a bag lady – what was her name? – had a quirky poem about a hand-to-mouth, independent life in a studio apartment on 86th Street, but there was nothing pitiful about her. Patty and Lois will always be in my life, Olive, no longer in New York, has be-come a novelist (I see her name in reviews). The 86th Street woman is lost to me. That night we are all brand new.

In the weeks to come, I will learn important things from Judith: that we will write best when we're encouraged and feel good about our writing, that critiques should begin in a spirit of camaraderie, that we are good poets, the future poets of our time.

I am high on that thought when she cautions, "By the end of these six weeks of writing competently, your job will be to stretch to greater distinction, to a uniqueness that rises beyond competence." Oh.

My friend Rosalind has invited me to dinner. Having become an artist, she moved to New York City from Chattanooga almost two years before I took the sublet, and she wants me to meet two of the creative people now in her life. She wants me to know other writers.

Down South we were first introduced to each other as two women who should meet. Friends of ours must have sensed that each of us needed more than Tennessee, that our unfulfilled desires might be compatible. Though both of us had husbands and homes and young children when we met, we had chosen to have other lives as well. Not usual in our circle in the sixties.

Our initial meeting took place at a beauty parlor, *Moda Tienda*, after a shampoo and set. As we were about to be placed under dryers, I heard Rosalind's forthright voice and sensed a connection. Now that she and I are out from under that weekly ritual, we laugh at how it brought us together.

Most women we knew were living full-time mommy-wife lives with some volunteer, charity work on the side. Before the Women's Movement no one called housework work, unless you were a maid, nor was it even seen to be a choice one made – it was simply the life a girl was expected to live. As the southeast director of the Experiment in International Living, Rosalind was immediately different and stimulating to me. She was out in the world, flying to attend meetings, living in other countries for weeks at a time. I knew only men who did that, and few of them.

Having married without finishing college, I was going to school to get my degree, which was also unusual. Before continuing education became part of the college curriculum, I, in my thirties, was the oldest student in every class. When I met Rosalind, I was about to graduate, class of '68; soon I'd be teaching language arts at Pine Breeze, a Chattanooga high school for emotionally disturbed adolescents.

By 1981, Rosalind has gone beyond the Experiment to become a world-class photographer; she's gained a name among artists and museum curators. Now here we are, both of us in New York City.

When I walk into her apartment for dinner, I'm the first guest to arrive. "Eve Merriam is coming," she tells me, excited, since Merriam is a writer whose poems and a play about women she knows I admire. "Not for the whole evening, but at least you'll meet her."

Rosalind is experienced in the ways one pursues a profession, and she wants me to succeed in this world of accomplished people as she has. Our backgrounds are different; from the start she's had privilege and wealth which she detests as bourgeois – her struggle will be to escape it – but it has given her ease in high-powered social situations which I find uncomfortable.

I go toward the windows to a fabulous view: the fountain rising in the center of Lincoln Center, the Metropolitan Opera House with Chagall's windows in the distance, Balanchine's ballet company to the left, the Philharmonic to the right.

Audrey Wood arrives, and she's immediately engaging, full of lively conversation. A small gray-haired woman in her eighties, she is the theatrical agent who brought Tennessee Williams to Broadway. She asks me how I know Rosalind who has just photographed one of her clients, the great actress Eva LeGallienne? I stammer something weird: "We were housewives together."

Just last week I saw Le Gallienne perform, and here I am,

making conversation about a legend whose life I have walked into. With Audrey Wood, a woman who has helped create legends! This is certainly not Chattanooga. In a year I will feel part of theatre history when I know that I saw a diva in her final role. And in ten years I will consider it daily life, normal to be living in the presence of talented people, sharing their work. But at this moment I am obviously gaga.

Not normally an actor's agent Miss Wood explains, "How could I not represent her? Of course I said yes after Miss LeGallienne's dear agent died and she called and, in her words, cried 'Will you take care of me?'" This warms me, to know how artists will reach out to each other.

Audrey Wood has had her assistant, a young man named Patrick, drop her off at the party on his way to the opera. "He's probably an opportunist," she says about her new employee when he leaves, "but at my age I don't care. He amuses me, he makes me laugh."

Ms. Wood introduced Rosalind to Eve Merriam, thinking the two of them might collaborate, photographs and text. Merriam enters in a bright pink, down coat. It's the first season for stylish down, and she looks so lively in it, chic and bubbly. She is sixty-five years old, her face lined like my mother's was when I thought her old, but there is nothing decrepit about Eve. I'm the mess.

Am I sitting right? Should I have given her my seat next to Audrey Wood? Should I have stood when introduced? I had decided to be low key, to wear dark pants and a maroon wool top in a new T-shirt style. I'm not feeling formal enough, or do I mean clever? Everyone's so at ease, such lively diction, so many charming anecdotes.

Merriam excuses herself early – "To be with my fella," she says. "He's just flown in from California." She says goodbye to me and tells me I must call, our apartments so close, mine on Perry, hers on 12th, come for a glass of wine. How kind she is, how she makes me feel like a peer.

Naive, I'll be surprised when, after I take her up on her invitation, she calls on the day we're to meet to say something's come up, and she has to cancel. It will take me a while to learn the pace of New York City life, how little room one has for simple visits.

When we're ready to leave Rosalind's apartment, I offer to drop Audrey Wood at her hotel, the Royalton on 44th Street, on my way downtown. In the taxi she continues her stories, how, when she started as an agent, the head of the new drama department at Yale invited her to New Haven to see the work of young Tennessee, and she had to go up the night before, take a hotel room which was very unusual for a woman in those days and she a girl of only twenty. I am listening to her the way a child, open-mouthed, is transported by storytelling, awed by what feels otherworldly, yet instructive.

Gracious, inviting me to call her, to come by her office to see the photograph of Miss LeGallienne that Rosalind – "so talented" – took, Audrey Wood thanks me for sharing my taxi.

"It's my pleasure." I hear my polite and clear reply, then wonder if I should have jumped out to help her exit, to help her up the steps to the hotel; I watch her totter for a moment before she stands upright and elegant.

One month later, on the way to a Robert Bly reading at the New School, I will hear from Rosalind that Audrey Wood is in a coma from which she'll never recover. And today I am older than Eve Merriam when she entered my life in pink down, and she too is dead. I am alive – how can it be, the time, the way it goes – walking on their footsteps.

"Will I see you again?" I ask Judith Sherwin when the Y workshop is almost over. She suggests we have lunch.

I take the subway to Central Park West. Judith's doorman calls up to say I'm here; she tells him she'll be right down. No last look out those windows.

"What kind of food do you like?" Judith is deciding on a

restaurant as we head toward Broadway. And when I hesitate, because any place with her would be fine, she suggests Chinese. "We like it," she says.

Such a little remark. But to me, the moment is ambrosia. I am taking this casual walk toward Broadway with a famous poet who wants to match my desires with her family's choices. At lunch Judith suggests we order noodles in sesame sauce when I say I've never eaten them. It's new to me, this attention to details, to the food we eat, to everything we do.

We talk about the way a poet makes community. I have hinted I want her friendship, and very gently, wisely, she tells me about peers, nothing to do with age; she is speaking about writing.

"When I began to write," she explains, "women such as (and I hear names I do not know since I am just beginning to read contemporary poets) were beginners like me, and we are still friends, exchanging poems. You must create your circle from those who are where you are, your writing peers. And hope to find someone – teacher, writer, editor – to respond to your work. When there is such a meeting, the result is the attention we all seek."

That instruction moves me beyond mothers and fathers to sisters and brothers in the new family I will come to choose.

Sure I got to choose my husband, but I was very young, a teenager. Home and marriage, living under one roof with the same person year after year, left me longing for who and what – outside and inside – would step toward me if I had waited and spent time alone. Straight from my parents' house I made a home with Harold. Though I went away to school for two years, I lived with others in dorms but never by myself. Always roommates. In 1953 I knew no women who were living by themselves.

A woman defined herself by marriage. It wasn't a choice she

weighed, nothing like "Maybe I should wait, become a ___,"
or "I wish I didn't have to." For me and my friends there was
absolutely no desire or decision more important than husband.
Though I didn't say that, the thought was there like the air one
breathes. A girl (we never used the word woman) asked, which
man do I want, how do I get him?

Harold, my first date at the University of Texas in 1949,
was the man I was waiting to marry. He was a senior and I a
freshman. On that first date we went dancing with a group of
his friends. I could see people liked him, he was easy and out-
going. Two nights later he listened to me tell the story of my recent disappointment, that the one college I'd wanted, Sarah
Lawrence, didn't want me. He listened! We were on a cook-
out; he cooked, he showed me his way with steaks. I was to
open the can of Tater Stix, and I sliced my thumb on the tin. He
cut my meat.

The year after he graduated, I talked him into giving me his
college fraternity pin. We turned it into a ring and called it an
engagement. Three years later, discharged from the army to
which he was drafted during the Korean War, home from Japan
where he was lucky to have been sent instead of the warfront,
he said he needed time, or whatever. I say *whatever* because I
couldn't see that it mattered, his job uncertainty, his lack of
money to live on. I said we could figure it out together. We'd
had sex which in those days meant I was his, he was mine. But
we didn't talk about that.

The summer before I'd been offered a job teaching at a local
county school: "I hear you're real smart, Miss Myra," the principal of East Side School had said, introducing himself to me on
the main street of our small, southern town. It was 1951; I was
nineteen; Harold, twenty-four, was in the army. "I need an
eighth grade teacher when school opens next month. How
about it?" I said yes because it seemed more exciting than going
back to the university. And I was waiting for Harold to get out

of the army so we could get married. Playing teacher had been my favorite childhood game. "I can do that."

So while my husband-to-be was in Japan, I stayed home, in Dalton, Georgia, and taught eighth grade, all subjects, to future Abraham Lincolns and their future helpmates who had to drop out of school for six weeks each year to help with the cotton farming.

My students and I liked each other; I cared about what I taught. I'd say, "Make sentences with the words you're learning to spell. No point in spelling *distinguish* if you're never going to use it." No one had spoken to them in such a personal way, wanting to connect them with the excitement of learning; and the boys and girls, some of them close to my age, caught my concern for them, my love of words.

I didn't hear from Japan often, but when Harold returned from what he would often refer to as the best year of his life, I told him, "It's time." What I'm sure that meant is "It's time I start real life, marriage."

As my first date at college, the first boy I slept with, the first male who made me feel comfortable, he had to help me begin. Harold was like a brother I must have felt I could count on. But a brother without introspection, not someone who mulled over decisions to be made; at least he didn't express deliberations, so he seemed a person who knows what he wants and acts. Every other boy had been careful of my reputation (a key word in those days), which meant in sex you went only so far. Necking, petting we called it. Harold went all the way, without talking it over. We just did it. And I didn't know it was going to happen. Of course I couldn't tell anyone.

So after the army it was time to insist, "You have to marry me now, I can't wait anymore."

He'd gone to Florida to work for his brother-in-law. When he continued to balk after my many attempts to convince him by pointing out how long I had waited and by showing him

budgets on paper of how we would manage, an alternative plan
from who knows where popped into my head. The next time
he called, before a weekend together, I decided to let him off the
hook. "If you're not ready to get married in February, I can go
to New York City." I said it with newfound, genuine joy. After
graduation from college, a friend of mine, three years older,
had taken an office job in New York with Revlon Cosmetics; I
could move in with her and her roommates.

Harold, who is a born negotiator, must have sensed he was
about to lose me to a suddenly surfaced dream. We set the date:
February 15, 1953.

Marriage Ann.

The dream of New York was genuine although I chose to live
the other dream which convention placed before me in 1953.
I married. Then marriage or domesticity didn't really satisfy
me. I tried to be domestic in a romantic way, fussing over pretty
dinners, cooking what I thought Harold liked to eat although
I'd never had an interest in cooking. In the Florida town where
we lived I couldn't find a job so I didn't quite know what to do
with myself besides read, and where was that going to lead? I
didn't know how to talk about my discontent. I think I began
to feel like a person incapable of happiness, a rotten kid growing up to be a miserable adult.

In 1981, finished with childrearing, and very lucky to have the
Women's Movement as guide and new convention, I have pro-
ceeded with my alternate dream. People tell Harold, "She just
thinks New York will make her happy; she'll see, and mean-
while she'll get it out of her system."

Alone and anonymous, I am a poet in the City, and everything feels right. The past no longer makes me bitter; it's as if I
can turn memories into something sweeter through my writing.

I am able to give myself a future in which I express the past. I can be philosophical, enjoying Kierkegaard's line: "Life can only be understood backwards; but it must be lived forwards." In a kind of heightened, confident present, I walk into a restaurant and pretend others are looking at me, wondering *Who is she?* Sometimes I purposely choose a fancy restaurant and occupy a table for one, imperious as royalty, high on independence.

My mother, who never handled a checkbook, was given money by my father to run the house, but she was savvy enough to keep money aside, to hide it for her private pleasures. I'm sure she wasn't different from most housewives who had to account to husbands. I can remember very few practices she felt it important enough to instruct us in, but she warned my sister and me to be wise: "Always put aside money that can be yours alone." I have come to say the same thing about time and space, the necessity of putting aside mine alone. Each day, everywhere I turn in the city, I am free to take in the world around me and, alone, experience it. I find it wonderful to be filled with energy from others who do not require my response.

As my teachers have suggested, eavesdropping feeds the writer. Privy to an endless supply of good stories, in elevators, on buses, standing in line for tickets to a movie or for cancellations to a play, I simply tune in and receive the world.

When spring comes, I open the windows of my sublet and wake each morning to the fragrance and buzz of people gathering at Lanciannis for coffee and croissants. Aware my stay in New York will soon end, I relish everything all the more.

One night I decide to eat at Trattoria da Tavalda Calda on Bleecker for the roast chicken they stew with fruit. Two middle-aged women with stylish short hair, one a redhead, the other blonde, perhaps Upper Eastsiders downtown to enjoy the charm of the Village, sit at the next table, but only one talks, on and on, about the sacrifices she makes. The other nods or grunts her understanding, or sighs in compassion. The talker *into*

has just confessed her endless martyrdom: "What can I do? I'm into social justice." I love it. To be *into* is a new expression, and here it is, used in all seriousness, and mine to enjoy, her devotion like the joke circulating these days about the Pope's being *into* religion.

In line for a cancelled ticket to *Childe Byron* at the Circle Rep Theatre around the corner from my street, I'm behind two young couples. When the very thin mate of one goes to the bathroom, her partner talks about her to the other couple: "She's so emotional. This play will make her hysterical; that's what I had after *Tess*. She was so upset by that movie she took it out on me, all that happened to Tess. But it's because she's so sensitive, so fragile."

And the other woman, listening, inquires, "Where's she from?"

"Jersey," he answers.

The play is not as good as the eavesdropping. Afterwards I amble along Seventh Avenue. It's a balmy night, people are out in great numbers, charged, sensing summer, smiling. I mix myself with the others, walking in the direction of Sheridan Square. I'll browse in the lively corner bookstore. Inside the store, I stand next to two men in their thirties who are schmoozing in front of a shelf of current novels.

The one in a T-shirt is telling the more intellectual-looking man in wire-rimmed glasses, "We're married but I mean it's not a marriage. She didn't take my name and there's no ring, and if she decided she wanted to leave she knows she could; I mean that's it, I wouldn't give a shit. But we get along really well and we've been together now a long time."

He wouldn't give a shit though they've been happy, together for a long time. Oh, this is a new world. He surely doesn't hear what he's saying, but he's got the ear of his friend, and mine, with his bravado.

"Giving a shit" enters a remarkable dream I have later that

night: A young knight appears before I wake. We are dancing. When a piece of his armor protrudes from his breastplate, I push it down to be closer to him. And it is perfect, our fit, the warmth and ease of our dancing. Then I go to the house of my childhood and read a note on the door about proper attire, wearing a girdle when I wear a tight dress. I see people out in back who may want to keep me from my knight. Has something happened to him? I stand waiting, thinking perhaps they are digging graves. But when I walk up the hill, my father and younger daughter Judith are digging a swimming pool. It's then I hear barking and look up to see a lion emerging from the hillside. Amazing, a beige lion formed and rising out of the beige land! I run. How can we live so close to a lion in a suburb? Inside, upstairs in a large room, I am sitting on the toilet. The knight and Judith are working, hammering something on the wall. I am shitting and shitting but trying not to let on. It comes and comes, and I try to be inconspicuous as I wipe and wipe. The knight, smiling, asks why I keep sitting. I say I like to sit, I say I'm thinking. Finally I get up, have to wash the shit from my hands; I hope all the paper will flush. I see an egg on the floor with some of the shit on it; I wash it clean. The lion is still out back, half in, half out of the hillside.

What a dream! That lion, and my knight – is he my night? – this new life of solitude, of sleeping alone, of dancing with myself, my muse in armor. Yes, and I love the proximity of armor to amour. Past and future are there in my father and child, my history and promise. Busy shitting I'm ridding myself of what? Then I remember my eavesdropping, the man who said he wouldn't give a shit if the one he was happy with left him. In my dream I am giving a profuse shit. It is on my hands, on an egg – which is my new life, my poems? The beige lion, half-in half-out of a beige hillside – am I stuck? and poised to go forth?

It's a powerful dream I wake from on the morning Harold

is due to arrive for another weekend. Waking to the egg I am
washing clean makes me feel protective, like a mother of her
baby. And fully awake, I think maybe it's my apartment I want
to protect.

When Harold arrives, he has a business appointment he's
set up. I have much of the day to myself. But I can't work, my
head hurts. I can't find what to say to my body to soothe it.

This apartment has become my workroom. It's not an out-
of-town getaway or neutral territory anymore, and he is in it.
I try to ease into my work by reading. I open Rainer Maria
Rilke's _Letters to a Young Poet_. Turning the page I notice my
hand smells bad. There's shit on my wrist. I can't believe it and
it frightens me. Maybe I need to ask Harold to help me, I mean
to love him, to ask him to love me. Oh shit! No wonder the lion
is stuck.

What does follow my strong dream is a poem, revealing
what I had never before expressed, about my life, about my
muse as male:

I have had to wait this long to make a castle
out of sand, to let you amuse me,
to find each of my fingers kissed
for being there. It's a simple story – I was born
to a man and woman so besieged they could not love.
When I learned to read, then life began
in and through a book. Opening a mystery
I called out the name _Shirley_
penned on the flyleaf. My mother shrieked,
my father ran to me, closed the door, whispered
the story of their daughter dead at 11 in surgery.
They had never wanted another
he said. He was simply telling the story.
I was 11 when I opened her book. I couldn't die,
or it would kill my mother so I lived

carefully right – excelled in school,
married, gave birth. Then I was 45
and Mama died. She couldn't lose me anymore.
Only then did I write poetry, only for you
my dark brother, my nighttime dancer.

Summer, 1981

Tennessee

JUNE 1981. Time's up. Linda is back from France to re-claim her apartment. I return to Chattanooga. To keep life coming I'll have to have poetry. And it comes out of the hills of Tennessee to meet me.

There is to be a poetry workshop in mid-summer at Van-derbilt University in Nashville, just a hundred miles away, led by no less than Marge Piercy. Her book, *The Moon Is Always Female,* sits at the ready on my desk in case I need a dose of "For the young who want to":

Talent is what they say
you have after the novel
is published and favorably
reviewed. Beforehand what
you have is a tedious
delusion, a hobby like knitting.

The concluding couplet I'd memorized: *Work is its own cure. You have to/ like it better than being loved.*

Immediately I sign up for her course. The week before I drive up to Nashville, I dream the lines *I came/ I soared/ I cuntcurred.* When I string the words across three lines in my journal, I'm embarassed, yet happy that my dreams give me word play, as if insisting Poet. I'm confirmed, let it come.

At Vanderbilt it's good to be in a room alone again: my bed, a desk, a chair: my own place for five days. In the evening, at the student center set aside for our workshop, I run into people I know, a guy from a Lit class at the University of Chattanooga and someone I met years later. As I socialize, talk talk talk, with overbearing men and self-effacing, southern women, I feel my energy go. I'm left with an emptiness, but I can't keep quiet or stay simply attentive, clear and calm. A guy says, "Save me from one more poem about mothers." And I add, "Or grand-mothers." I'm joining him in his derision! The more I chatter, trying to fit in, the emptier I feel.

Next morning when we meet Marge Piercy, I am relieved to be genuinely engaged by her ability to listen, her eyes welcom-ing, taking in our words. She is simpatico not only in age and politics but also in the writing schedule she establishes for our days. We'll work alone mornings, then attend class in the af-ternoons. It's wonderful to stay in bed working, to go from dream to drift to waking. Seamless time I call it.

Some of us form a group outside of class to respond to each other's work. "Erasing the Color," a poem which today I don't even remember, draws the sort of support that makes me note: "The group thought the poem strong; I'll keep working on it." It's what I often find: reading a poem aloud, bouncing it off others, lets me sense its strengths and weaknesses. Now I am centered, back in a community of poets, and the week goes well.

In our last class Piercy tells us it's tough to be a writer ex-pressing the mean/ angry/ questioning/ erotic side of ourselves as we continue to face family. She tells us not to fear: "A mu-sician cannot hurt with her music."

I swallow the sentence, especially the startling her of it, the use of that feminine pronoun to generalize still new to my ears. Like an adolescent I'm ready to break out, to feel my strength, to grow into this world of accomplished women who write. "For the Young Who Want To" is not age related Piercy has told us.

At the closing banquet Alex Haley gives the keynote address. It's a series of anecdotes surrounding his bestseller *Roots*. Marge wants wine, and none will be served; we're in the Bible Belt. Another woman and I go to her room to bring Jack Daniels, Tennessee's finest, back to our table. We've poured it into soda bottles, and we offer it for the pleasure of those around us. Afterward, walking back to her room, Piercy complains: "How could he speak without one idea? How could he dare?" I would think she'd give him more slack, be glad the school has asked him to be the guest speaker, but I can see she refuses to be condescending; to a good writer words always matter.

In her room we talk about the writer Grace Paley and the anti-war movement. When we mention Women Strike for Peace and the War Resisters League, I talk about my cousin Sophie in the Bronx, her politics, how in her house I took in, along with the food around the kitchen table, the idea of a world made better for the working class. I think of the poet Audre Lorde and mention hearing her read in New York, how struck I was by the word *empowerment* which I heard for the first time from her lips.

It's time for us to say goodnight. Marge wants to take a bubble bath with her favorite fragrance; I can't remember what scent it is, but the fact of a favorite bath oil, the strong femininity of it impresses me, that we don't have to be ashamed of ourselves as women who love beauty and sensuality in order to be powerful. Saying good-bye, she hugs me close. I've never had a hug like it, holding another near as if to feel the earth of her body. Its fullness has come to be second nature to me, the only way I know to hug now, a form given me by Marge Piercy.

On the way back to Chattanooga I make little poems in my head. Of Paley and Piercy: *The two of you hold/ your bodies to the ground/ in the same round way.*

Arriving home late afternoon, I bring in the mail and open a thin business envelope from the New School in New York, thinking it an announcement for the upcoming season. The letter tells me I have won the 1981 Dylan Thomas Poetry Award. A check falls to the table. $200. I begin to sob, my whole body beyond itself with joy, with who knows what release of pent-up life.

I reach for the telephone to call Harold at his work. When he hears my impassioned sounds, my voice unable to speak words, he panics, "What's happened, what's wrong?" I must steady myself to tell him what I've received.

He's thrilled. He'll try to come home early, we'll celebrate. What he mentions to others first is the check for $200. To him, a businessman, it confirms my accomplishment. He has never called my writing a hobby as his accountant has, and the word dilettante is mine, not one he uses, but for both of us this recognition gives my New York dream a solidity from which to go forth into a new time.

Second Sublet

The Upper West Side, 1981–82

WHEN MID-AUGUST CAME, a month after the Piercy workshop, Harold and I flew to New York for a long weekend. Though we were vacationers in a hotel, we felt like insiders. Even our daughter Judith was part of the city now, as a summer intern at an art gallery. I chose a hotel near Central Park; I wanted to walk from where we slept to Joseph Papp's Shakespeare in the Park. As if I lived nearby.

And I soon would. With a lead from a friend, I was in direct pursuit of a sublet on the Upper West Side, a large one-bedroom in a rent-subsidized building on 90th and Columbus, owned by an older couple who wintered in Florida. This time I was not an actor pretending. And this time Harold was with me.

I gave references (Linda from my Village sublet and Gary, a friend from Chattanooga, who now works for the *New York Times*), and I mentioned my Dylan Thomas Poetry Award from the New School. To these old-time New Yorkers I had the right credentials. From the African masks and Mexican prints on their walls and the political books on the shelves, I could tell I was in the house of extended family. Their apartment would be mine for eight months, until the end of May.

When October arrived I moved in, and a new side of the city opened for me. What one calls New York City, even Man-

hattan, is a conclave of neighborhoods, and if you were blind-
folded in a restaurant in one neighborhood, then taken to another, you would be able to guess almost immediately which
part of the city you were eating in by looking at the people
around you.

I knew right away the Upper West Side was not the Village;
I looked out the window at families; streets were filled with
children playing on the sidewalks. Lining my street were high-
rise apartment buildings and a school a block away on Columbus. It felt like the Bronx of my early childhood, before my
father moved us South.

Remembering that sublet now, I can see myself the first day
there attending to the ritual of making the apartment mine by
going room to room, looking in each drawer, on each shelf,
shifting the too-muchness of a lifetime of furniture and arti-
facts into closets to make room for me. Then I'm out on the
streets, walking the neighborhood, along Columbus up to 95th.
It's an early, balmy evening, and I'm in a world of many His-
panic and African-American families. I stop for dinner at a
place called West Side Story.

In the restaurant the manager welcomes me; Joni Mitchell
is singing "Both Sides Now" on the sound system. There's not
an empty table in the house. I take a seat to eat at the bar next
to a man who smiles when I tell him I'm new here, just arrived
from Tennessee. He tells me he's from Utah; he's a fiction writer
though he makes a living practicing law.

I look down at the book he's reading and express excitement at seeing it's by Loren Eiseley. "He spoke at my college
graduation! I was so pleased to have a writer, such a good one,
at the University of Chattanooga. I was lucky; he was a friend
of the new president."

"I'm a huge fan of Eiseley," he tells me, "how he writes with
passion for the natural world and with such a gift for story, the
way he describes holding the point of a pencil in a spider web,

watching the spider adjust to the change." I'm in heaven listening to this man I've happened on over dinner in my new neighborhood. I'm home, North, going back and forth about books, free of the place where you're confined to driving to people's homes for conversation, where you hardly meet strangers or have chance encounters like this.

Walking back to my sublet after dark through streets of tall apartment buildings that are not charming, not cozy Greenwich Village brownstones and cobblestones, I tell myself it's what I must embrace this time. This is not last year's ooh ahh euphoria, this is feet on the ground, eyes straight ahead, and in back and sideways. This go-round I'm no longer the freshman New Yorker.

In the morning my friend Patty calls, she, the poet of everyday images in our Judith Sherwin workshop. (I still remember the mayo on a BLT.) She's been accepted to the fall workshop at the Writer's Community.

"Have you?" she asks. And when I say I haven't heard, she assures me, "I know the secretary, I'll call and inquire."

Whatever the outcome I'm here supported by poetry friends. They care about what happens to my poems, I mean they hold my words close enough to be able to describe them (to the secretary). Patty identifies me by "Hair," how in that poem I used a particular word as prayer. That a poem of mine has entered and stayed in someone else's mind is new, is love to me.

Before I left Chattanooga to take my first sublet in the city, people questioned where I'd find friends, others my age not already attached, ready to make room for me. They didn't know New York. In this city nothing is set or unchanging; people make friends through their involvements, no time for either constant attention or aimless chit chat. Friends I have today I met in workshops; we liked each other's poems; we were excited to grow, no matter our age, through our love for poems and writing.

Ing. A writing friend, Ingrid, takes the subway from her house in the East Village to visit me in my new sublet. Petite like me, she's thirteen years younger, tough and affectionate like my favorite cousin Sophie. I look to Ingrid for guidance; I trust the way she lives in the city, connected to politics and family and writing. We have tea in my living room, as if I've been here for years. At dusk we look west, out the big windows, toward Broadway and the Hudson River where the sun is setting.

This year I face one of the few vacant lots across Columbus Avenue. In December it will be filled with fir trees for sale. The snow falling will create a twentieth century, New York City holiday scene, and I will sit at the window, watching couples load their Christmas trees into the trunks of taxis.

I've just read about a woman who gave herself to the contemplative life of a monastery where the work of each day was *Monastery* to pray, not to change other people or assume responsibility for them but only to work toward one's own urgencies, in order to achieve the power to praise. In this cloister there are skyscrapers to press up against; life glows around me; silence and anonymity encourage something hidden to emerge.

L‍ast sublet I did not arrive until January. This time I will be part of New York in the fall, and at the end of this month, on Halloween, Patty and I have arranged to meet in the Village, on Bank Street, right around the corner from that first sublet. We want to watch the Halloween parade which, I'm told, is a ritual for Village people.

IN GREENWICH VILLAGE ON HALLOWEEN WE TALK
OF LOVE

Dearest H., you'd have roared and carried on; hearty
laugher that you are, you would have clapped to see

such happiness. A high-heeled man in a silver sheath
threw chocolate kisses; a woman, wrapped paper leaf,

uncurled, became an undulating tongue of green snake –
and an old man who leaned as if to kiss my cheek
coughed golddust in my face. All night I sparkled.

But what I started to say, before the parade
got underway, had to do with love. The way

I love you. Waiting for the hoopla, I told my friend
I love you as the shore the wave. Set to marry

in December she wants to talk of love, what we
two do that's lasting. I said I love your going out
and I know you're coming back. As simple as that –

as putting on your robe – don't laugh – to be a nun
parading with a book, with women friends in sisterly

devotion, always knowing there's another, a man
(you) who gives me something else – less intensity?

touch, release. Fun – but weird to think of ordinary
love that way – right there on Bank where we once fought
about the first apartment – so scared we'd separate –

Because all my new friends are writers, I feel for the first time
I am choosing my birth, where and to whom I'm being delivered, a harmony I crave in contrast to my childhood. When I
was nine years old, in 1941, we moved from New York City to
a small town in northwest Georgia. Being yanked from place to
place was not new to me; the only centeredness I'd felt was in

my cousin Sophie's apartment in the Bronx where she lived with her husband, their two children, and her parents, my Tante Annie and Uncle Morris. Their house was our refuge, where we ended up when we were evicted and once when we found bedbugs in the middle of the night. Sophie's house I always find pleasure in remembering. There, everyone gathered around a table to eat and talk, to organize protests and make the world better. There, people laughed at jokes and sang Yiddish songs. There, a bookcase held the complete set of the *Book of Knowledge*. In my mind the shelves were arms encircling me, holding me while all the adults were busy. I cannot remember any of our own four walls. Asthma and arguments I remember, trying to breathe while my parents yelled. And I remember fighting fiercely with other kids when I went out to play.

We moved to the South for my father to have a steady job managing a chenille bedspread factory in Dalton, Georgia, the Bedspread Center of the World. It was calm but far away. We had a house my father returned to each night, to my little sister, Raina, six years younger, to me, and to my mother making dinner, a world like Dick and Jane's. To make that happen something had to go: my moxie. Like sap from a tree. I had to learn not to yell, to have good manners.

I remember the principal leading me to Miss Huff's third grade class that spring, walking into the room while the boys and girls were singing. Some of the words are still with me: *Welcome sweet springtime, we greet thee in song. La la la la la birds float on the ay-er. Ay-er* is the Yiddish word for eggs; that it was the southern word for air I had to learn. I had moved to a strange place with a foreign language. *Yes ma'am.* Never *huh*.

My hair was long, blonde curls like Shirley Temple's. The girls in my new class made a fuss over me, which was also a wonder since no one ever had. They said, "We're going to put on a play about Sleeping Beauty and we want you to be her."

I was so excited, and I could see that my mother was happy

too. She washed my hair and, with her fingers, shaped each platinum curl. The next morning she twirled them again. I was ready. Then the girls told me they looked in the back of the book and found out Sleeping Beauty must have short, dark hair. I knew there was no such back of the book, but here I couldn't fight. I sensed girls in this place never did. I had to play dumb so they'd play with me. (The sonuvabitches!)

I had to learn many different ways: my new friends had church to go to and the country club to swim in when summer came. Coming from a Jewish Marxist family I was puzzled; I'd never seen the inside of a synagogue much less a church, and in New York we played in a playground. The twenty or so Jewish families in Dalton decided to form a synagogue in an old house that became a social center as well. That's how it was, social life had to do with your religion; no Jewish people belonged to the country club. As I grew into my teens, the other Jewish girl my age and I would go to Chattanooga or Atlanta to meet other Jewish kids. During the week, at school, no one talked about these divisions. I learned to be quiet.

In 1981 in New York City I am past childhood, past the confusion of a place never really home to me. I feel I have stepped into *my* life. Marriage, its domesticity, my own house, never quite fit. I used to live with an airplane fantasy. When I was car pooling or sitting in my children's dance classes, writing down the dance steps they had to know for their recitals, or when I was walking down the aisles of the supermarket, I daydreamed about a gateway that led to an airplane that would fly me away.

In this new sublet to which at last I've flown, I marvel that these mornings are happening for me. I wake and always open the blinds to look out at the street life below. There is a stable on 90th Street and often I see people on horseback, riding toward Central Park. Then I start my routine, reading poems in bed before breakfast. I'm rereading Randall Jarrell. He and Robert Frost were the poets I loved most in my English classes at the University of Chattanooga: Frost because he wrote poems in which husbands and wives struggled with their differences, Jarrell because his poems in the voices of women expressed my longing, in particular, his "Woman at the Washington Zoo." In its last lines the woman pleads with the vulture she watches: "…step to me as man:/ The wild brother …/ You know what I was,/ You see what I am: change me, change me!" Her plea was mine.

In our college texts almost no poems by women appeared, and Jarrell's women were a gift. Years later I'd come across lines from Sylvia Plath (in "Getting There") and Adrienne Rich (in "Orion") that told me they too were deeply affected by Jarrell's poems. This morning, as I reread Jarrell, the domestic misfit I was rises, bringing tears. How did Jarrell know, in "Next Day," "my wish/ Is womanish:/ That the boy putting groceries in my car/ See me. It bewilders me he doesn't see me."

Married at twenty I exposed myself to another before I opened to myself. And when I had a baby at twenty-three, I was a baby having her. Who was I with someone else to keep alive through my body? Just that, a body hungry for – and that I didn't know. I didn't seem to have a maternal instinct or a natural desire to housekeep. How in the world could I know, in the middle of another's desperate hunger, what I craved? I loved to read but I called it escape, thinking I was losing, not finding, myself.

When Karen was born in 1956 we were living on the north side of Chicago where Harold had taken a job, and I was happy to be in a city. She was born in March, so until the snow melted I mostly stayed in, too tired to read, watching soap operas or sleeping between her feedings, with no natural pleasure in what we had created. I remember becoming hooked on an afternoon soap opera, *As the World Turns*, and though I recall nothing of its story, I can still see the woman in a mink coat from one of the commercials. She was there to demonstrate the beauty of pink *Dreft*, a detergent she poured with great flourish into her washing machine just before leaving for somewhere interesting. Next time at the grocery I bought it.

I knew I was supposed to count my blessings; still I yearned, where was my life? In the summer of that year, another mother I met in the park, wheeling our babies – buggy friends we were called – mentioned going back to school in September, and, while our husbands baby-sat, we signed up for a literature course to get out of the house one night a week. Instant joy!

For eleven years I was a college junior. It began with that first class, Victorian Literature. That's what was offered on Tuesday nights. The Brontes were not included, but even Thomas Carlyle made me happy. Each week school became my party; I counted nickels and dimes buying groceries to save enough for a baby sitter in order to read and write some days at the library. Professors praised my intelligence; *you write like a man* one noted on my paper. In those days we took that as a huge compliment.

All through the following years I never let myself take more than one course a semester, for fear of finishing. Without awareness, and until consciousness came, I did not know how joy would appear in everyday life without books and school.

FEAR

Time to leave the past and my bed. My Upper West Side sublet is one block from Central Park; its rolling paths, bridges, and lamplight are the setting in the dream I'd remembered when I looked out the window that first night at Judith Sherwin's workshop, yet I miss being in the Village. On Tuesdays I walk through the park to the Lexington Avenue subway to go

downtown to attend a poetry workshop – no registration nec-
essary – with men and women I have never seen until we walk
in from the night street to St. Marks Church in the Bowery on
Second Avenue, no one asking our names. Each week all we
know is that we're writers, here together.

Beginning a new workshop excites me the way new semesters
always did, and now I do not need to squeeze pleasure into baby-
sitting hours. It's hard to take my good fortune for granted, and
I continue to be afraid the bell can ring to say it's over.

As the autumn days proceed I begin to read the poems of
New York poets. I reach for the poetry book lying next to my
bed that I bought at St. Marks Bookstore, coming from Maureen Owen's workshop at the Church. It's her book, *Hearts in
Space*, in which she writes, "'Trouble in the air,' Amelia Earhart
noted, 'is very rare./ It's hitting the ground that causes it'",
which makes me laugh, thinking of my old airplane fantasy.
Only now I'm overjoyed to be on the ground with Maureen
Owen at St. Marks. Her writing is exhilarating – "& You O
Bald October/ I knew you when you still had hair!" These days,
in Central Park, the sun is shining through the bald spots, and
the weather is so mild I can sit on a bench and read, then write
about my midnight taxi ride:

…past twelve I roll into a cab
and get a prince
who knows the speedy way
every light is ours
and while we fly
he tells me of his weekend
in the Catskills, he names
the colors leaf
by leaf: scarlet maple
russet oak, white ash
purplish as wine

Going to a poetry class in New York, even when I am the oldest in the group, is good. Two workshops at a time is better. Once, in a workshop, a poet called me docile. "In the best sense of that word," he said. Until I looked it up in the dictionary, I couldn't imagine *docile* as a description of me, the bossy one, the planner, the child who'd kicked and screamed. "Capable of being taught," was a definition I found. Yes, that's me.

During this fall term of my second sublet, once again I'm in two workshops. In addition to the one I walked into at St. Marks I've been accepted for a class at the 92nd Street Y. Gerald Stern is the poet leading it. His book, *Lucky Life*, so affected me last year, I began to write my own poems as I read; he's the first poet to whom I ever sent a fan letter. That was the month before I arrived in New York for my first sublet, and he'd answered with an invitation to breakfast. We'd met briefly at a restaurant in the Village on Sheridan Square. Immediately I felt comfortable with him, his rough voice, the way he dressed, knit cap pulled over his balding head; he had the working class look I'm used to. As we said goodbye he took my address for a book party Houghton Mifflin was going to give him when his next book, *The Red Coal*, appeared.

It had felt remarkable to be recognized as a poet by him, his telling me the poetry community was a small one so we would meet again. And now he's teaching one of this semester's poetry workshops at the Y. When I first made inquiries, I'd asked Shelley Mason, the new director, about him, raving about his poems, how moved I was reading them in Tennessee, this Jewish, wise man's voice inspiring me to my own, giving me courage to begin writing at my age. Although Stern has been writing all his life, in his sixties he's just beginning to get major recognition for his work. *Lucky Life* is only his second book.

This workshop at the Y is his first teaching stint there. The class is taking place in the building, unlike last term in Judith Sherwin's apartment. When I arrive for the first session, there

are ten of us. I remember the joy of gathering with poets when
I met Patty and Lois. This year we sit around a table; Stern tells
us to distribute our poems. The writers are all new to me. I
hand out my poem, "The Cadences of Southern Kindness":

When I tried on the woolen sweater
coarse ribbed wool
and the salesclerk gushed
How Sweeet!
my stomach pitched
back to the April of my greenhorn days –
kinky-haired outsider, brassy kid
brought from the Bronx
to a rosiness as puzzling as thorns.
Caught at hide and seek I spit
You sonuvabitch!
to who was It, and every kid
shrank from me, stopping play.

I had to whip my words
with air. They said
say ma'am to get **sweet** milk
at lunch, *may I ma'am?*
to use a **rest** room. But *huh?!*
was all I knew.
Sweet milk turned out to be a carton
of plain pasteurized
and later when I ran to rest
the room was dark green rows
of sinks and toilets
the Spring my father's powerful hope moved us
South to make a buck.

Immediately Stern says it's good. Of course, I'm thrilled; I brought it because it's an important poem to me, but there are line breaks I'm unsure of. Someone comes up with a suggestion, then Stern takes over with a theoretical discussion about southern gentility and language, how it serves to keep out Blacks and Jews. I'm interested, but I begin to get very nervous; I can't listen because he keeps talking – there'll be no time for suggestions from others, there'll be no space for their poems. Finally I say, with southern politeness, that we should move on, that I'd like to hear more, maybe later, and he says "Yes, on the couch."

Angry, disgusted, embarrassed by his remark, I don't answer. All I can do is keep my eyes down. After class a woman calls him a vulgarian. I don't know what to think. The southerner in me does not want to confront; the Bronx kid is used to his kind of earthy vitality. I continue to attend the workshops. I tell myself last semester's class spoiled me; I was like a baby being nurtured. This year I have to grow up.

For our last class in December, our group, which has dwindled in size, decides to meet at someone's apartment. I say, "Come to my place." The day of our meeting I'm returning to New York from Chattanooga. I take a morning flight. Fog has settled over the Chattanooga valley, and we are bussed to Atlanta, arriving just in time to make the connection to La-Guardia. Outside New York the pilot discovers there's trouble with the landing gear, the flaps aren't operating properly. We head for the JFK airport where the runway is longer. As we land, fire trucks wait, but we're in and we're safe. It's late. By now a morning flight has become one arriving late afternoon. There's traffic and the taxi driver says it's bad all the way to the city because of the rain. Possible snow. I won't be at the apartment when the group gets there at six thirty. Will they wait for me in the lobby?

When I arrive, after a seventy-five minute taxi ride, it's six

forty-five, and they're waiting! My whole body, bracing, can let
go and I'm giddy with gratitude. We enter the apartment together. I'm so glad to be in its warm mix of masks and fabrics.
Since it's late we get right to work. For our last session I'd
wanted to make egg nog in the spirit of the holiday, but I don't
do anything. I can tell people have places to get to. Stern gets
up in the middle of our distributing poems to make a phone
call. That takes a while.

In my joy and surprise at having made it out of the airplane
alive, through the bad rainstorm back to the poets waiting, I'm
manic. I know I've expressed my joy excessively – "It's so good
you're here; I'm so glad to be listening to poems," chatter I can't
control when I'm nervous. One of the poets tells me I don't need
to say thank you one more time. Before I can respond to him, a
woman says, "It's feeling. Myra's overcome by feeling."

It's then Stern says, "There's an effusive woman in the office
of the Y who says 'God bless' constantly, and it's an expression
I hate. She always smiles, always goes on about how good it feels
to be out, working, singing, dancing after having raised eleven
children. Whenever I hear her and her 'God bless' I feel like saying 'Fuck you.' 'God bless' is arrogant. Better to say, as my father did when gentile people came into his store and sneezed,
'Ess dreck,' which is Yiddish for eat shit. 'Thank you,' they'd answer, assuming he'd blessed them. 'Ess dreck,' that's something
real." Stern then adds "Why do women need to gush so?"

I realize his story has followed my being told I didn't need
to keep saying thank you. I stand in a daze, reeling from the
story and my whole day. We've finished going over poems, and
everyone gets busy saying goodbye and happy holidays.

At the door Stern turns to kiss my cheek. "Happy New
Year," he wishes me. Out of my mouth it comes: "*Ess dreck.*"

Stern is taken aback. So am I. Others laugh. Then I close the
door and lean against it.

The kid from the Bronx is back.

After a holiday vacation in Italy, just the three of us, Harold, Judith, and I, Karen in Los Angeles deciding not to join us, I'm back in the sublet. Since reading guidebooks is a skill I have and enjoy a lot, and Italy was so richly beautiful to explore, I was happy. It was our first trip to Italy, full of sightseeing that ended in Rome where we watched 1982 fireworks light the sky from a restaurant on top of the Spanish Steps.

Harold has flown back to Chattanooga, and after he calls, I phone an old friend, Francine, a New Yorker who now lives in Connecticut. I know she's in the city to visit her parents who live around the corner on Central Park West. I met her in 1956, the year Karen was born, and we've been through heavy history together. We agree to meet for dinner before she leaves town.

On my way to the restaurant I think of how much Francine was part of my life before the Women's Movement, how much she was the joy in it. Before Betty Friedan's book, *The Feminine Mystique*, which was published in 1962, I simply couldn't see how to create a life beyond wife and mother. The fact that I loved literature and school, that I'd worked as a teacher before I married, should have led me to consider teaching as a profession. It didn't. In Friedan's book an explanation came as the title of her very first chapter; I along with thousands of educated women were living the problem that had no name.

When I read *The Feminine Mystique* in the late sixties, words came to fit my life, to help me rescue it, not just escape it. Suddenly there were many women to share my story. We sat together in circles. Consciousness-raising it was called. We came to discover the ordinary as revelation: we and our daughters could act according to who *in particular* we were, we could come out from under the one role of marriage. If my life came most alive through books (even guidebooks), I should consider work that would embrace that passion. A profession.

I remember Gloria Steinem and Florence Kennedy coming

to the University of Chattanooga. In the student center we
women sat around them as they asked us about our studies and
aims. When one woman said she wanted to be a nurse, Flo
Kennedy said, "Say doctor and I'll give you my Angela Davis
button." No one had done such a thing, elevate our dreams.

It took many years before I realized I could change my life
without a man's making it happen. I had developed what I'd
come to call my Elizabeth Taylor fantasy: to change a life a
woman changed her husband. Liz Taylor, who was born the
same year as I, had been married twice by the time she was
twenty. For years she was the woman who knew how to make
life evolve; time after time she simply married a different kind
of man, each one opening for her the next way of being. And
in the early sixties that's what I'd figured I had to do, try to
find another man, a college professor, a man who would get
me to a book-centered, literary life.

In 1956, three years after I'd married, I met Francine. We
shared, to perfection, a rich fantasy life. I'd never met anyone
else who could match and nurture that blissful side of myself.
And she was a New Yorker. Walking to the restaurant to meet
her, I think back sixteen years to 1966 when I had traveled to
New York to visit her. One night I ended up staying elsewhere.

"Is it snowing where you are?" she asked when she called
the next morning. I looked out the window of a stranger's
apartment in the Village on Charles Street and answered, "Yes,
the rooftops are white."

She said, "Look down. What about the streets? We're not
going to be walking on the rooftops." Always clever, her wit
was a gift I defined as sophistication. We laughed. She, my best
friend, was coming to meet me for lunch. I'd phoned her after
the man – what do I call him, her friend? my lover? – left for
work. She'd introduced me to him; we'd all gone out for dinner at La Strada, the four of us: she and her husband, I, her
friend from the South, and a man they'd met on a recent vaca-

tion when they'd celebrated the new year, 1966, together. They liked him. Newly divorced and on holiday with his children, he had been glad for their friendship. I say they liked him. It was really Francine, her flirtation she was playing with when she gathered the four of us for dinner.

She says I was the one who first talked of affairs. I think it was she. Or maybe it just grew in mid-air out of the fantasy life we built from books and movies, our books more real than our lives. They were our recipes for how to proceed now that the lock-step of school life no longer existed and what we'd aimed toward, marriage, had become our lives. We'd write down passages from books that seemed essential, then put them in our purses to instruct each other. Because I'd fallen in love with the poet Randall Jarrell, his "Woman at the Washington Zoo" ("The world goes by my cage and never sees me"), I'd brought the poem to show Francine; its last lines would thrill her too: "You see what I am: change me, change me!"

Francine had named her daughter Nicole for F. Scott Fitzgerald's Nicole Diver in *Tender Is the Night*. I'd seen the actress Judith Anderson play Hamlet and gave my younger daughter the name of a dramatic, gifted woman. How else to enhance our ordinary lives? We were not domestic, we were literary heroines.

For me Francine was pure New York City which meant everything intellectual and vibrant. I remember thinking, "If something happens to Francine, if she dies, I'll die." I realized she was the only person whose life would mean that kind of loss to me, my soul's mate.

When I first met her, Harold and I were living in Chicago, up from the South for a job he took. I was eight months pregnant with Karen. Francine, the month after her graduation from Sarah Lawrence, had married a Chicagoan, and we were introduced at a couples' club party held after a Friday night synagogue service. The way she tells it, an enormously pregnant person leaped across the room when she heard New York and Sarah Lawrence and immediately asked, "Will you be my best friend?"

That was her patter – you had to love hyperbole and I did, taking giant steps to catch whatever she threw. Our friendship held fast when, three years later, she and her husband moved East and we moved back South. Our husbands took new jobs, and we, who were the wives with the children, followed. I'd get to New York when I could, and once she came to visit us. A world traveler, she had never before ventured below the Mason-Dixon line. "It's the most foreign place I've ever been," she told her husband on the phone, "no one knows Flaubert or Fitzgerald."

And then, under the influence of Madame Bovary, or despite her, we began to push the envelope. I don't remember who went first. Was it she with the rabbi, the one we called Judaism's foremost scholar, because he was, or me with the new professor at the university thirty miles north in Tennessee?

On a snowy morning in February 1966, she was coming to hear about my night with her new friend. This man was perhaps the key to my future, a new life, how I would change the old one, how I could get myself to the City that would make me come true. I simply didn't know how else to change my life, how, unless I did it with a man, I, a woman with two children, could make something new happen.

I came again to New York to see him. And, of course, I shared my drama and plans with Francine. She seemed upset and, I sensed, jealous. I was confused; she'd put the two of us together.

If, twenty years ago, I were writing about this, I might want to analyze Francine, but what looms now is the snow, and how it caused me to confront my life, my marriage. Harold had planned a business trip to Chicago when I said I was going to New York to visit Francine. I'd left the day before his trip. The children were home with a housekeeper. During the night it snowed, fiercely. He couldn't fly; he had to take the train, the Georgian, to Chicago and, there, make his way by elevated train to my sister's house in Evanston. It was an adventure he wanted to tell me about so he called Francine's house where I was supposed to be staying. She made up something; she said I'd call. By the time I did, Harold knew I was with someone else. Did my sister, who knew about my affair, hint? Did Francine give me away with her voice, a hesitant excuse?

When I called Harold he was waiting by the phone. "Myra," he said, "don't lie to me. I know you're not at Francine's. I'm going to call you there, I'll wait an hour."

I had to make up my mind. I wanted to defy him, but I didn't want to stay with the other man; I wanted time. We drove to Francine's house and waited for Harold to call. He did; I didn't confess anything. Where I would end up I had to figure out. Harold says what hurt most was my not saying "I'm sorry." But I couldn't, I wasn't. I did, however, know I had to choose.

It was messy. Even after Harold knew, I kept seeing the other man, and lying to Harold, and making a life out of that drama: flying by day to another city, back home by dinner, the secret post-office box. Harold hired detectives – one opened the door of a hotel room to take a photograph, and I, the Bronx kid, the fighter, stared straight into his camera.

Harold confronted me, "If you want to leave, do it. But not with the children. You won't take care of them."

Harold was acting on an attorney's advice; together we went to his office for instruction. The lawyer said, "You should start deciding how you'll divide your property." Property included the two children. When we left the office we went out for dinner, and we laughed at the lawyer's notion of property; in our laughter was connection. Is it possible that because of one word I stayed? I stayed.

It wasn't a matter of one true love. From a childhood of arguments between my mother and father, I find disorder hard to endure. And true love hard to give. I'd never witnessed it at home between my parents. I knew I wanted a life I didn't have, and I failed to know what that meant or how to get it. Unlike me, Harold could feel accomplished in the business he was building. As I write, I believe there must have been something at the core of us that knew our temperaments and values fit to make a good life together, yet in order to proceed we needed order in our lives; we needed to be able to struggle through our differences; we needed time and the ability/luck to remain together while making it happen.

I stopped seeing the other man. We spoke on the phone a few times, and then the calls stopped. Francine eventually left her husband to marry him. During the years of their marriage I never saw him and hardly saw her. He died eleven years later, before I took the first sublet. Harold and I and the children went on together, wounds and all. I went into therapy; eventually Harold did too. Elizabeth Taylor and I parted ways. And by the seventies, women's liberation took hold in Chattanooga.

Tonight, all these years later, I enter the restaurant to meet Francine, aware that she was once my green light, the promise I needed to feel alive. I learned to turn on the light without her, that I am the light.

Walking through the door I see her in her black leather jacket, early as always, waiting for me. We are quickly seated, and she is all questions: How are the poetry workshops? Am I meeting exciting people? What have I been reading? She is curious and supportive and neither of us mentions those threads of our history that bound us in 1966.

It happens one Monday, holiday spring term '82, when I'm back in Chattanooga for a week. Late afternoon the phone rings, and a woman who won't identify herself, except to tell me that she works for my husband, wants me to know my husband's making out with one of his supervisors. On the sofa in his office.

I hear myself refuse to be thrown off guard. "His business is his business," I say. At the same time I want to hold her on the phone. As if I'm in a soap opera, I want details. I know to say little, that my silence will keep her talking. At one point I do announce I'm shocked. When she hangs up, she says, "Thank you."

Lentil soup on the stove is boiling. I take it off the burner. I feel cold so I warm my hands over its steam. And I feel relief. I'm not the bad one, the one usually acting out. Humor. Curiosity. I feel that too. What will I do? Since I am seldom moderate, can I believe I will stay cool? My only visible signs of emotion are these shivers.

My mind makes pictures. I fasten on his office sofa, the pumpkin and blue classic design, spirals on a white background I helped choose. Knoll wire chairs with blue cushions to the right and left of the heavy, round glass table. On the wall a painting I always disliked of a woman in a white gown lying on a sofa. I said she was painted wrong, she'd never be able to sit up.

When Harold comes home I don't mention the call. But I say her name, I can't resist wanting to speak of her, "the other woman." There's no reaction from him, nothing to titillate. I realize I'm not good at indirection, but I can't or don't want to confront. And I don't.

Next morning I'm heading back to New York. Changing planes in Atlanta, I hear someone call "Myra Stein." Yes, that's me, in my maiden days. It's the voice of a man who remembers me from Dalton High School. He invites me into the Delta Crown Room as we wait for our flights, and over tea he tells his business associate how I was the smartest in the class. Charles Bramlett – what a sweetheart to appear at this moment.

When Harold dropped me at the airport I began to feel the

furies rising. Suddenly angry and insecure I wanted to turn around, to go back home and wait there to pounce. And just as suddenly, someone hands me school, my past glory. It pushes me forward. I walk to my New York flight like a public figure, important to the world, the anonymous world with a smart Me in it.

When I arrive at the sublet there's a message from Robert Brown, my friend from last year's class at the New School. He's reminding me we're meeting for dinner before we go to Jill Hoffman's winter workshop we decided to take at her house. We have several poems we're working on, so we'll have a chance to share them with each other before we join the whole group. After we eat, and I read a new poem, Brown says, "What made you cry at the lines 'the bed we've shared for thirty years, the same bed/ for thirty years'?" He's a New York friend, a friend who knows to question. I don't even have to answer. But later, when I think about those tears, I imagine they came from the child in me that would have wished always to be the only one desired.

After the workshop, which goes well – Jill Hoffman, a tough critic, liked my poem, the luck of that – I take out my secret. I picture the woman in Harold's office, her bleached blonde hair, her strength, her shrill voice. She's a small-town, southern version of me, defiant, energetic, and competent.

I don't call Harold as I usually would, to say I'm here, the flight fine. In the morning he calls me, and I find myself digging. "What time will you be home tonight? Should I call so we can talk, since you're rushing out to work?"

Coolly he answers, "Eight, eight thirty, no need to call. Is there anything in particular you need to tell me?"

Now I'm angry. At her, the manipulator, the cheap trickster. But I don't say any of that. We say good-bye. We have our needs, my mind rushes to tell me. I think of what I did before I made it to New York and poetry.

I never found out if Harold had an intimate relationship with someone at work; it was as if parity meant my freedom, his freedom.

That I owe this life to the women's liberation movement and a therapist was the luck of being born to my generation and not before. That I was able to save myself through them may have to do with my proximity to the values of my cousin Sophie's family, their love of the arts, their strong sense of community, and their heartfelt attempt to matter. When, in the seventies, a new friend who'd moved to Chattanooga from Colorado had said, "Let's start a chapter of NOW, the National Organization for Women," I agreed and we did it. In one year, 1968, I'd finished college and a year later applied to the graduate school I wanted. With no master's degree in English offered in Chattanooga, and on the advice of a professor who had his degree from Middlebury College's Bread Loaf School of English, I traveled to Vermont for six weeks each summer from 1970 to 1973 to earn my M.A.. Which meant the children went to camp, Harold to his work, and I to a superb education in literature. I had only dreamed of the likes of Ted Taylor from Columbia University teaching me *Paradise Lost*: "Look at the first lines of a work, how what follows fulfill them;" Bart Giamatti from Yale noting in his book my observation of death inside love (mort in amor) in the fifth canto of *The Divine Comedy*; Robert Pack reciting Robert Frost in the very place Frost had spoken his poems. One day when I came a bit late to Pack's class, he asked someone sitting in my usual seat to move. And though I was embarrassed, I reveled in knowing that I had a certain place and he needed to see me there. It was four summers of heroic work – it was glorious!

When the possibility of going to Vermont first came up, I thought my therapist might think it extreme, a fantasy, that

I was running away again. But he knew, of course, go, and I went: to poetry, to my life waiting for me without a man. At the time I couldn't believe the world could so simply yes my desires.

In New York, by the second sublet, I know I am on my proper path, but I am struggling with confusions about my writing. The workshops are not quite satisfying, and the newness of being with other poets is not automatically the wonder it was when I first arrived. I continue to meet writing peers from Colette Inez's and Judith Sherwin's workshops so that's good, but my poems aren't.

One night after a laborious class at Jill Hoffman's, working on a poem up until it's time to go to her house, I have a startling dream about the poet John Ashbury. He's put his hand in my pocket and asked if I minded. "No," I say, "it feels good." Then we start walking to catch a plane, and I can't find the Delta gate. I ask a couple of people who point the way through the ladies room, which I'd tried but it seemed a dead end. I try again, and again it leads nowhere. Somewhere along the way I embrace Ashbury and say, "I wish I were a boy." Eventually I seem to be holding him upright; later I say I don't want to continue to do that, let's hold each other up. Then, when we are lost and can't even see the airport, I see a big, athletic guy running. At first he doesn't see me, and I wonder if he's dangerous; like a shadow he blends into the night. Twice I ask him for directions; he points the way and points again around a curve, and I see the airport lights.

I tell the dream to my friend Brown when we meet for dinner, and he remembers our talking about flow in poems, my poems lately in stanzas that look like boxes. "Maybe it's a message to run with the language," he offers. But I want to talk about welcoming the boy, at first through a gay man, then an athlete. I figure I need my dark brother, my nighttime dancer. For centuries the muse has been female – maybe the muse is male when a woman is the writer? My dream had me off course until the athlete points the way, which makes me think of my circuitous route to poetry, how I didn't write poems until my mother died. And though I am grateful for a friend like Brown, I feel distant, a slight nausea which is rare for me. It has been that way for a few days.

dream

The next day I wake to a feeling of deep sadness. I make Cream of Wheat to soothe myself, and I open Galway Kinnell's book of poems, *Mortal Acts, Mortal Words*. I begin to feel better. At least I'm not nauseous or nervous. But what is my sadness? I can't figure it out. It's nice to know that tonight I am meeting a group in Brooklyn to work on our poems.

sadness

On my daughter Karen's birthday, I wake up with the same sadness, a heaviness I can't explain. For the past two rainy days I've been working well. Today, in the sunshine, I'm down. Karen is in Los Angeles so I wait to call her. I call Harold; we talk about the day she was born, and I get teary. When I phone Karen I try to make a celebration by retelling her the story of her birth, how the days of being taken out for dinner she's mentioned mirror the many days she took to be born, how we marveled at seeing our cleft-chinned, beautiful girl when she was held up to us; but after I hang up the phone I feel I generated a kind of false warmth. I chattered; I didn't let her talk.

Later in the afternoon, meeting my friend Ingrid in the East Village to see the new studio she's rented for her writing, I can't rid myself of sadness. When we go to a café I order tea and put the hot cup against my forehead. Ingrid reminds me I'd felt sick last year at this time, "Isn't it in March that your mother died?" Then I realize it was five years ago, the weekend of Karen's twenty-first birthday, Mama died.

Mama's death

My head clears as if a jammed door had flung open. I start to talk about my mother, and Ingrid listens, lets me cry, holds

my hand. I'll always love her for that. And afterward I fly
across 10th Street to Sixth Avenue – the World Trade Center's
two powerful shapes standing south in the darkening blue sky
– as I satisfy a desire to buy shoes, an urge that must have come
from the memory of Mama's giving me her navy blue pumps,
taking them off her feet, when I admired them. It's a memory
I hold as one of the rare times I see her as powerful – she alone
had taken me to boarding school my first year away. Before
leaving me, she let me trade my shoes for hers.

When I get back to my sublet I phone my sister Raina to
tell her how Mama's death had revealed itself. "I love you,"
she says as she hangs up. And when Harold calls, concerned
about my sadness that morning, he is moved to hear about the
day full of love. I go to bed thinking of Ingrid's advice about ritual, a form one must create for acknowledging death. If I were
my sister, who is a wonderful cook like Mama, I might make
chicken patties. I'll have to come up with my own connection.

THRALL TO IRIS

And I was wrestling that mystery, when, muscling free,
memory lifted off from
where it hides. Today is March the 21st, today is the day
my mother dies
and each year I put three iris in a vase to recognize her – if I
forget her, like a siren
she divides me. My head had banged like knocks on the door
all ordinary morning –
I'd let the heat of a shower enter my face, my hair,
but my eyes
kept throbbing, my nose clogged (with no tension
apparent to me).
As a vacuum sucks debris out of a rug, the apprehension of
her death clears my life

without her in it. My largest towel in her favorite color, a
Florida fuchsia, wraps her
around me to dry and dress myself the way you dress a doll
and say "errands to do"
and you take her out on them – to the flower shop to request
from a man
the freshest ones which he goes into the refrigerated box to
give to you, tightly tipped, purply-
blue ones, and, as it is with iris, they rise by evening; throats
yellow hidden in violet
now extend, pulling you towards their light, and always away
from their center.

When I think of my mother, how she was taken across an
ocean, her immigrant life, the death of a daughter she had to
go forth from, her chaos the chaos of my childhood, I see myself living a life that will redeem hers. It is a mission. In therapy, early on, my struggle with the past began to present itself
as something I could transform with and through my children.
I could become the mother I would have wanted. It felt like
plowing, reforming the ground to make a beautiful, strong
something grow. I became both my mother wanting out and a
luckier woman who could find a way to make it happen. I
could create a life consciously chosen, and it would be a model
for my daughters. My children would not hear me repeat my
mother's "I have dreams in my heart, but…", her voice trailing
off on admissions of weakness.

To this day I do not know what my mother dreamed, except
perhaps of a different man. When my father died she had two
years of proclaimed happiness, dating different men, dressing
up, going out with friends. She said she certainly didn't want to
marry, but after one man, a widower who wanted a wife and
found one, left my mother, she felt abandoned. She became ill,

and, in the year that followed, she died. Living alone, going out to meet friends, dating, she'd said, "These past six months have been the happiest of my life; if this is all, I'm happy." And that was that.

At the age of sixteen she had married my father. It was a chance to escape her parents' house. I have a picture of two worlds: eastern Europe led by Tsars and Cossacks who ride terror over lives, and then America, the land of milk and honey. And tenements. My parents start in one world, my mother with her mother until there is money to bring her to America, her father waiting on the dock; my father hiding in a rain barrel to cross the Russian-Polish border, his violin his pillow.

In America they both want freedom and beauty: she, a life away from many families together and a bathroom down the hall with others always wanting in; he, to be dapper in spats, to succeed in an American man's world while dreaming and painting and writing. In Brooklyn, in lush, verdant Prospect Park, they meet. She was sixteen years old, my father twenty-one. She had a lovely voice and sang the song of their day to him: "When you wore a tulip, a bright yellow tulip, and I wore a big red rose." He offered to take her out of the tenement, bragging about being a college man, which in reality meant he attended the Educational Alliance at Cooper Union, a place he'd gone to learn English, a place still standing strong, only three blocks from where I now live. My mother, not an intellectual or revolutionary like her older sister's family, said "Yes." They married. He will come home from the store he manages to find her – so young, barely sixteen – playing jacks on the front stoop. And soon she gives birth.

They named their baby daughter for the movie star of their day, Shirley for Shirley Temple; for eleven years she was their only child. My mother, wanting to be out playing, could hardly make room for her, but she was an easy child. And talented. Look at the painting of Cezanne-like apples she left behind.

DEATH of a CHILD

She and my father painted together. I can see from her note-book she liked playing with words, taking big ones to find the smaller ones inside. *Stupendous* gave her *up* and *pend* and *soup* and *tend*. But instead of going on and on, she died. In surgery. I'll hear how my father tried to warn the doctor performing the appendectomy that she was allergic to ether. And many years later, after my father's funeral, perhaps beset by guilt at not being kinder to him, my mother will speak of her shame, remembering how she made eyes at that surgeon.

To these two I am born, not two years after their child's death. I have no memories of their joy in each other, only the mysterious sight of them in the same twin bed in the morning after they'd screamed at each other all evening. Whatever love they found must have had to do with sex, good love-mak-ing; she was seductive and beautiful, he was creative and vigorous.

That there had been a Shirley, that my parents had lived as another family before I was born, none of this I knew until I was eleven. It was the secret in the house, the death I was born out of, revealed to me when I went to the bookshelf one morn-ing and opened a book, a western romance, and saw the name Shirley Stein on the flyleaf.

"Who's Shirley Stein?" I'd shouted carelessly from where I knelt. My mother dropped a pot in the kitchen and ran to the bedroom, slamming the door behind her. It was left to my father eating his breakfast to come to me and tell me their story.

Six years after my birth, my sister Raina arrived. We lived in the Bronx in the building where our extended family, Sophie and her parents, lived. It was only after we moved South, three years later, that I recall a celebration for my birthday. Sophie and her mother, my Tante Annie, came from New York to visit us in Georgia the month after we settled. It was May, and for my birthday they brought me an RCA victrola in a blue carry-ing case. It was as if they'd brought me Broadway!

The joy of birthdays stuck. I do not let one pass without
wanting something special to happen. The year of my second
sublet, 1982, I am aware of my fiftieth birthday coming toward
the end of my stay. And in the mail one weekend a brochure
arrives from the University of California at Berkeley announc-
ing three weeks in Greece and Sicily with Robert Bly. It is to
begin the first week in May and end on May 21st, my birthday,
ten days before I have to give up the sublet. What a gift, I think.
Yes, this is how I want to celebrate.

When I see Harold I mention it. He says, "If that's what
you'd like, you should do it. But you know I can't. I can't take
off for three weeks. And it's not my kind of vacation, a poet...."
He doesn't finish his thought. I can understand his hesitation,
special occasion or not. Most of the poets he's heard at the university in Chattanooga mumble; they're academics with their
noses in the text, and their delivery is no recommendation for
an evening, much less a three week vacation.

"Robert Bly is different," I counter, assuring him that this
man is colorful, even outrageous, a warm, forceful, humorous
presence. "I heard him read at the New School and did a one-
day workshop with him, writing about onions. He walked in
with a big bag full of them. He wants you to be engaged by
poems; he's social, a man you'll like," I tell Harold.

"I can't do it," Harold insists. "But you should go, certainly,
if that's what you want for your birthday."

When I mention this conversation to a friend who knows I
don't hesitate to go places by myself, she asks a crucial question: "Do you want Harold on this trip with you? Is it important to you that he be there?" I think about her question. I
admit to myself, yes, I do want him with me. I want to celebrate my fiftieth birthday with him.

As I say this to my friend, she asks me if I've told him so,
and I haven't. When Harold comes home after work the next
weekend I'm back in Chattanooga, I say something I've never

said before: "I want you to be with me. I would like to be with you and have you with me on my birthday."

Shocking. To express devotion. To ask for love.

Harold agrees to come. "But I can't leave the factory for more than two weeks," he says. "I'll fly back to Chattanooga when the group goes to Sicily."

May 2nd. Waiting for the flight to Athens we meet some of our fellow travelers and the group's organizer from Berkeley, Lynn Kaufman. Robert and Ruth Bly I don't see until we walk up the aisle of the plane. You can't miss Robert, a tall, robust man with a shock of white hair. Ruth is also tall; she's attractive and I imagine a bit younger than he. We introduce ourselves. I sense his reticence, or desire for whatever privacy he can claim for himself and Ruth, and later discover this is their first vacation together since marrying only a few years before, second marriages for both of them. I imagine this trip as an escape from newly complicated lives, their combined children and responsibilities.

By the third night in Athens we've warmed to each other. After a late dinner a few of us from the group make our way into the Plaka towards the music at the Sisyphus Cafe. There, our arms around each other, we join the Greek men we've watched dancing in circles. We search our pockets for handkerchiefs to hold in our fingers between us as we dance. We are couples and singles, but quickly we become one family, and this night begins our celebration of men *and* women.

Harold, who often stands behind a camera, takes pictures only when he's too out of breath to keep dancing. A photograph of Ruth Bly, her head turned ever so slightly, light brown hair pulled back except for tendrils curling around her face, looking in profile like a goddess, will be Robert's favorite; he'll ask Harold for a copy of it.

from the natural world *objects*

Robert has announced, "In the morning we'll all do a writing exercise using an object from the natural world, so pick up something while you're walking around." Harold protests, "I'm not a writer," but at Robert's hearty urging, he does it; he takes part in the assignment and discovers feelings about himself (and his mother) he'd never before expressed.

Day after day follows in this remarkable way. One night in Naufplia, we leave the group to be alone with one other couple, the novelist Tom Robbins and a much younger, blonde woman, Andrea, he's met on this trip. Robbins says he signed up to go with us so he could get to know Robert Bly whose work he likes. I'm aware of his fame, Harold is not. I can tell it charms Tom that Harold is not literary and doesn't know him.

We've sensed Naufplia is intimate, hugged as it is by the sea and hills; our hotel stands on a hilltop high above the water. We walk down into the center of town, exploring side streets off the main avenue that faces the Sea of Argolis where most of the tourist restaurants front the sea; we're trying to find a place off the beaten track, and our noses lead us to just where we want to be. As is the custom, the freshly-caught seafood is stored in metal drawers which are opened for us to choose the fish we want; pots of vegetables warm on the big stove.

Harold, who is by nature social, a southern good ole boy, lends the evening a playfulness that dispels our differences; we become four wanderers caught up in the child-like pleasure of smell and taste and touch. Late, we make our way uphill to the hotel. Halfway, I turn toward the sea – *look* – and we catch the full moon spreading itself across the water.

The day we return to Athens we climb the Acropolis to picnic near the Parthenon and decide to play gods and goddesses, writing their names on scraps of paper we pick out of a bag to act out and guess who. I pick Dionysus and reach for strawberries from our basket, dancing, flinging berries until, with a handful I've crushed, I press them against Harold's face, then

Tom's. Harold laughs, startled. Tom sticks out his tongue to lick them. I am in love with this way of living in the world, the deep pleasure of shared fantasy. By this time, when we're ready to leave Greece for Sicily, Harold is hooked; he'll stay the three weeks. He's been proclaimed by Robert the Zeus of our gathering, our host and overseer. Robert says of him to the group, "Here is a businessman, a man who built a factory he's run for over twenty years, and he hasn't lost the puer in his eyes." When Harold asks for an explanation, he is deeply moved by hearing someone acknowledge the boy within him.

In the Athens airport, on our way to Palermo, Robert suggests we gather for a story. Circled on the terrazzo floor like campers around a fire, we listen to Robert tell a trickster tale, how young Hermes lies about stealing Apollo's sheep, charming his mother. As we fill the terminal with the camaraderie of story and our laughter, I look up at the other passengers who seem deprived, sitting in their chairs, merely waiting to fly.

The last day of our three weeks is the day of my fiftieth birthday. We're in Rome. I tell Harold I can't single out people from the group for a birthday dinner, the whole trip has been a celebration, and I'm happy to let the day be like other days. Harold says no, we should celebrate. That decision on his part is new, unusual. He grew up in a family that celebrated only religious holidays. Somehow this trip has led him to the importance of personal ritual, and his insistence on it warms me.

It is difficult to discriminate among those we've met, but I do. With Harold I choose five people next to whom I'll turn fifty: Robert and Ruth Bly, Tom Robbins with Andrea, and Lynn Kaufman, a playwright, about my age, and the organizer of the trip. Because place is always important to me, I pick a restaurant in Trastevere, an old working class neighborhood which my guidebook calls picturesque. I think its humble origins will suggest my past, and its poetry my future.

In the courtyard of the restaurant we sit near a fountain. A young man is playing his flute in front of the church. Olives and garlic and tomato perfume the piazza. Surrounding us are lovely old buildings and the beautiful medieval cathedral. Food comes to fill our long table. Then Robert turns to me, "I hear you've moved to New York City to work with other poets. Let's hear a poem."

No one has ever addressed me as poet, looking to me to produce a poem as one looks to the fountain to bring forth water. Called to meet that expectation I meet it with the first poem I wrote last year in New York: "Gloria, I'm here in your City/ Even rain stirs me to the street/ Late last night I took myself to the Lions Head/ And the city, my street/ Was gold...." I recite and hear myself give a little segue about city and suburb, North and South, as if this were a formal performance and I needed introductory remarks. I continue with "The Cadences of Southern Kindness." Gifts asked for, gifts delivered.

"I see you love the city," Robert laughs; "Harold's in for it." Everyone laughs. To me that *it* means not just the city but poetry.

For dessert a big bowl of fresh fruit is served with a bowl of water to wash it. Ruth whispers to a waiter and soon we have a cake with candles. Then Robert says, "This calls for a group poem," so we go around the table, each of us creating two lines of poetry to follow the two we've been given. All I can remember of that verse is how Ruth sings of the flute, and its sounds come through the fountain in harmony.

From Rome, the next day, we fly back to New York. And I'm home. We take a taxi to the sublet instead of another two planes to get us to Chattanooga. Harold and I are high from the extraordinary time we've just spent together, and that spills onto the city, making us happy in it together. Harold will fly back to Chattanooga the next day; I stay on in the apartment for ten days, until the end of the month when the owners return.

I keep thinking about Harold and me in Greece and Italy; for the first time, past children, we were creative together. I think back to our honeymoon in 1953 when I was so sure if only we were someplace beautiful, we would also become beautiful; free of routine and the constraint of others, we would give to each other our full and sensuous selves. I'd said we should begin our lives together on an island. And so I'd said Nassau, which in those days was exotic; one had to fly over seas to get there, and we knew no one who had.

"If we take only three days, with our wedding gift money, we can do it," I'd said, trying to fantasize out loud with Harold. He couldn't imagine why we should. His mother had given us her opinion, "But you have nothing, no furniture, no car, nothing, and you want to spend your money for nothing when the honeymoon is over?"

I didn't know what to tell her. And out came, "I must have poetry in my life," which stopped her cold. And amazed me! As a mother now, I feel for her, how she must have worried for her son. But it was a wonderful moment of absolute truth. Without any awareness, the poet I would one day become had delivered a message.

Harold and I argued about my need for an extraordinary honeymoon, and I understood that ultimately it was his decision. I couldn't force him to go to Nassau, a place he couldn't afford and no one he knew had been. I'd pushed him into marriage; enough was enough. And to avoid disappointment I must have abandoned my desire, because when he surprised me three days before our wedding with tickets for Nassau, I remember being caught in a state of mixed emotion. I must have had to resurrect excitement; I wasn't fully there for his present.

There are honeymoon pictures of us in Nassau: getting on the tiny plane in Miami, Lord Beaverbrook from London a fellow passenger, being welcomed with rum cocktails upon landing. I could hardly contain the thrill of this first trip *abroad*, the luxury of a fancy hotel, another culture, foreignness. Harold, who doesn't share my fantasy life (I didn't know to express that then), I can hardly remember next to me. Only our making love/sex brought mutual passion, but even so we experienced very little conscious play. Did we ever look at each other's body? After all the busyness of planning and going, an emptiness came that I filled with nattering and judgments. From that first day we discovered the terrible loneliness of two people who have chosen to be together, each one having abandoned a part of him/herself in order to be there. There and not there.

The photographs remain. In gray pedal pushers and a gray and white striped T-shirt, a huge straw picture hat on my head I hold down with my left hand, I am standing next to a horse and carriage, next to a Bahamian policeman, a bobby – so British! – in his white helmet. Harold is taking the pictures; I pose, he clicks. And on the huge green lawn of the hotel a buffet lunch has been arranged near where I sit, and Harold aims the camera to catch the celebrity near me, Ray Bolger, the dancer, at a table next to ours. Surely those photographs will testify to the beauty of a life, that we will be different from our parents, that we are living a life worthy of lovers in a book.

From our honeymoon we returned to Orlando with stories to tell of exceptional events. I tried to cook a festive first dinner out of the *House and Gardens Cookbook*, each step measured, questioning how much lettuce to shred for a salad, which the book did not answer. Harold, who worked for his brother-in-law at the Fleisher Family Shoe Store, came home at six thirty while I was still cooking and decorating the table with hibiscus flowers, and since I was nowhere near ready, he napped until nine when I woke him. He said the hamburgers were good, but I knew they were dry. The coconut cake with white frosting and pineapple filling was pretty and delicious. Both of us very tired.

When I began to figure out how to give us dinner more easily so we could eat earlier, I talked Harold into walking with me

to the library. I wanted him to see how peaceful you can feel in
the large room full of possibilities, how much fun it could be
to browse the shelves and read magazines from all over, and
then in the night air walk back to our own apartment on
Hibiscus Court, holding hands and the books we'd chosen.

MARRIAGE: FEBRUARY, 1953

The night before our wedding day I took
A fit. My mother, who said she hadn't cried
Like that when her first baby died, shook
Me – too many fittings? showers? – to take pride
In my fine man, in what I'd planned: angora
Sweater, dinners by candlelight, perfume
On my arms, White Shoulders, its aroma
Would take us to an island place, a room
Unknown, our very own. Pioneers. Married
I cooked, he waited to be fed. His work
Did not go well, we moved. Pumpkin-headed
I wandered aisles, staring. Pick up. Put back.
Spring. On Hibiscus Court hibiscus bloomed.
I longed to be back home, getting married.

The contrast of those trials to the joyful few weeks Harold
and I have just spent together, the way I have turned fifty, gives
me what matters: my threshold life, part of me in family, the _bridge_
other in a community of poets. Between them a bridge on
which I am learning balance. Now I don't push Harold into
being my library companion nor is he the only one I have to
walk hand in hand with. He doesn't have to carry that weight,
and I don't have to be disappointed if he doesn't.
    The trip to Greece has given me two-ness, confirming once
again how it suits me. I want two families. Like Persephone

drawn to the underworld by Pluton, living both below and above the earth, dividing her time each year, I have two houses to offer richness, inner and outer worlds, cave *and* construct.

I spend my last week at 90th and Columbus enjoying Central Park, and I walk to Madison Avenue, looking in shop windows. I even buy myself a pair of turquoise enamel earrings. My mother's pleasures, her love of clothes and jewelry, fabric and color, I am coming to imagine as a celebration of Aphrodite instead of a pile-up of *tchochkes* and glitz. After Greece I have a desire to be beautiful. Taurus-Gemini birth baby that I am, on the cusp of its two elements, I am aware of earth and air shaping me, both home ground and poetry. Calling myself a poet, I try not to be afraid that I am my father, the braggart. Somehow, in union with Harold, I redeem my parents; I have the power to unite them.

When May 31st comes, I give up the sublet, having planned ahead for family and poetry. Stirred by Galway Kinnell's poems, I've applied for a summer workshop he's leading on Martha's Vineyard in July. Words from his poem "Flying Home" feel like a blessing: "It is also good – and harder –/ for lovers who live many years together/ to feel their way toward/ the one they know completely/ and don't ever quite know,/ and to be with each other/ and to increase what light may shine…." His words send me forward to Harold, and to the summer.

Summer, 1982

Tennessee, New York and
the Vineyard

MID-JUNE HAROLD AND I go to west Tennessee for his niece's wedding, partying with the heavy drinkers in what feels to be a spiritless, desperate community, but I'm filled with our trip to Greece, and I feel strain but not resentment.

As the Chattanooga summer proceeds, the strain grows. Once again comes the sense of I can't breathe, *nothing moves*, of death. It becomes more than a metaphor when Harold tells me about going to the hospital near his work to visit the wife of a business partner. She apologizes for the mess of her room, the floor full of dead skin, her body peeling from psoriasis. The nurse bathes and oils her. Harold gets a broom to sweep up the dead skin. This image remains as an emblem of Chattanooga life.

Dead skin. The itch to fly away. I'm sinking. But buoyed by the knowledge that I have arranged for us to stay in a friend's house in New York, at the end of Long Island, for one week in July, I am not desperate in the old way. I have also made the plan to go from New York to Martha's Vineyard for my two week poetry workshop with Galway Kinnell and Sharon Olds. By now I've learned not to let too much time go by without a poetry community; even an experience as vibrant as our trip to Greece and Sicily fades.

Lucky I was told about the workshop last spring. I'd heard good things about Kinnell as a teacher (I've learned to ask about that, not just rely on the poems). And in reading Kinnell's poems in *Mortal Acts Mortal Words*, I'm taken with how his work brings domestic life to poetry. That's not usual for a man. Sharon Olds I don't know. Her one book of poems, *Satan Says*, I haven't read.

July can't come soon enough. I'm reading May Sarton's *Journal of a Solitude*; in Sarton I find a friend who expresses exactly my desire for an inner life. I try to write; Harold and I go out with Chattanooga friends, but there is no one to talk to about poetry. By the end of June I'm feeling endangered; Harold and I are arguing, growing distant again. I'm edgy about the momentum of my work, how I catch fire from Bly, from poet friends, then kind of lose it and sit on my energy. I'm drifting instead of turning ground. I keep getting sleepy. I'm back to the old habit of living for the future, planning ahead.

At last we're up north. On Long Island, as I prepare for the Martha's Vineyard workshop, I discover I've lost my poems. Did I forget to put the packet I'd prepared into my briefcase? Did I leave it on the plane from Chattanooga? I don't panic. I tell myself I'll arrive at the Vineyard like Odysseus washed up on the shore of Phaeacia, naked, just before he's finally home. He has no belongings, but the songs he sings from memory will mark him.

I reread Kinnell's poems. Start from there, I think, start from "Fergus Falling." Fergus is Galway's son, a name from Yeats. In "After Making Love We Hear Footsteps," Fergus "in his baseball pajamas" comes to the bed of his parents – "this one whom habit of memory propels to the ground of his making." I find comfort in the way Kinnell makes a life to connect poetry and family.

I wish I could relax this week, in this lovely Long Island

house with a garden, but I keep thinking about my own household and our children: Judith in New York City working at an
art gallery, living in a sublet infested with cockroaches; Karen,
working for a fly-by-night music producer in Los Angeles, pick-
pocketed on Rodeo Drive last week. They're coming to visit
for the weekend, and I need to get food and make plans. I'm
worried about them; I want us to have a good time together.

My body keeps switching from confusion to the comfort of
reading Kinnell. As glad as I am to be here instead of Chattanooga, I realize I've upped the ante since my first sublet. Now
I need more than a good location; I want poet friends and poetry.
If I can work I can love. I pick up _Mortal Acts Mortal Words_
again: "I want to be pahoehoe/swirled, gracefully lined." "Ah
me!" I breathe a deep, hopeful breath.

As I sit on the deck, reading, I run my fingers through my
hair, responding to a movement. A bug. I knock it loose. What
is it? The spider crawling on my open book? So small but en-
gorged and round. Arachne, the weaver whom Athena turned
into a spider. Has she been eating me, is that why my head
ached? I squash her and she's full of blood all over my page.

Because this death scares me, this murder, I promise myself
that each day I will ease my edginess by looking beyond myself
at something in front of my eyes. I'll practice observing closely
the most ordinary things, note how a flower folds, a radish
smells, tastes, feels; and after I've lived with what's outside me,
then I can go inward, compare it to my mother or someone
dear, make a circle to myself. This way of working I learned
from Robert Bly, how he had us write each morning in Greece
and Sicily; in this way I can continue to keep him standing by
me. He is my first teacher of _Pay Attention_.

I've arranged to drive to Martha's Vineyard with Brown, my
young friend from the Colette Inez workshop at the New

School and Jill Hoffman's group. I think about how we became
friends over his poem "Swimming to England," dear to me a
son's fears, writing about his father whose head bobbed far out
in the ocean. I remember staying after class to talk to him about
it, smiling at the fact that his name was Robert Brown, *almost*
there in the canon. Earlier this year when we took Jill's workshop together we became good friends.

Our decision to go to the Vineyard arm in arm, Bronx and
Brooklyn, *two mavens to the Haven*, we say, also has to do
with birthdays. Brown is turning thirty as we drive; he knows
I celebrated my fiftieth in a grand way, and he wants to hear
about it. He's a big believer in birthdays, making them signify
as I do. So we talk about what's coming this year in our lives. We
talk about poetry and men and women and sex and therapy
and even birth and death, a back and forth of comfortable, intimate conversation.

In the hold of the ferry carrying us from Woods Hole to
Vineyard Haven, I listen to the *shshsh* of the sea. Brown is on
deck. Sitting inside the car alone in the double row of cars, I'm
glad for the quiet, for the humming ferry. Somehow I don't care
at this moment how the island looks. Or the sea. I feel at peace,
sloshing in this warm place. Something good is ahead.

Brown and I have dinner together after we register for the
workshop. I'm eager to settle into the room I've been assigned
in an old shingle house. The room is spare, not charming, but
I love its position in the upstairs corner, and its shape. It has a
small alcove for sleeping, jutting out from a larger room which
has the table where I'll work. My bed is surrounded by four,
screened windows I open; everything is clean and in good re-
pair: a painted, tan chest behind my bed to use as a nightstand,
a funny brown rug for my feet. On this hot, sticky night, with
the shutters open and the windows pushed wide, little breezes
of salt air come through.

The next morning Galway Kinnell lectures briefly. He wants

our work to be shameless and fearless. He wants only new work. I'm thrilled, having come naked to this shore. I'll go to Olds certain days, Kinnell others. By the time two weeks pass, we'll have worked not only with both teachers but with all other members of the workshop. Right away I'm impressed with Kinnell's gift for making community.

The heat is palpable. This is an old-fashioned summer, no air conditioning. I feel it on me, a sensual, heavy force. I've dressed in the briefest top, my new burgundy, sleeveless leotard and pale lavender cotton skirt. When a breeze does touch my sweaty arms and chest, I'm caressed. On this island of tree-lined streets, even in this heat, there's the sensation of constant flutter, leaves rustling near the ever-moving sea, so different from the stillness of Chattanooga, very alive.

Mother/ wife

I feel responsible for Brown's thirtieth birthday so I announce it to elicit celebration for him. But then I can't stand the way I continue to lock myself into this caretaking role. I must get with women. And get to myself. In social situations, being with women gets me out of wife. And women around my age relieve me of mother. Mother/wife experience I've got; a new power I need. Last night a young woman I met assumed I taught in elementary school when I mentioned being a teacher. That made me furious, made me think I come off only as a nurturer. She'd better wise up!

After Galway's workshop I talk to a woman in the room near mine, Frannie. We look alike; she's short, her hair blonder, but our eyes and skin coloring are pale in the same way. She seems strong, with good talk; I watched her stand firm last night when she spoke to the one married couple staying in our house, insisting over the man's wishes that the key remain in a particular spot near the door. She's a New Yorker, tough, smart, kindred. And she's near my age. Not thirty-one year old Kathleen, fashionable, romantic, seductive, who hates getting old and losing innocence, not college student Cynthia, good

poet for whom Galway's face beams boyish in admiration.
Where's room for me? I want admiration too.

I need to work. I choose to walk alone, take the long way
around to get to the center of town, to pay attention to what
calls me. I pick up a pine cone, its brown layers like the shingles
of these island houses I'm becoming fond of. I like the continu-
ous folding, one over another, the layering. Shingles are New
England, both old and new world, I muse. A thread of wood
extends from the tip of the pine cone, beyond the stem, like a
long brown whisker. If an owl had whiskers it would be like
this. I think of my father and how I loved to watch him shave.
Since I feel I'm more my father's daughter than my mother's,
his energy mine, his excitement and his writing, I think of
Athena born from the head of her father. And her animal is the
owl! Amused, I'm off and running toward a new poem.

Before I go to bed, I begin to read *News of the Universe*,
Robert Bly's anthology, subtitled *poems of twofold consciousness*. I brought it with me because of my attention to two-ness.
Immediately it speaks to me with an aphorism written in 1798
by Novalis: "The seat of the soul is where the inner world and
the outer world meet. Where they overlap, it is in every point
of the overlap." That's my pine cone, that's me and my pine
cone. I'll turn it into poetry.

And then, after five days on the Vineyard, I go dancing. I
join a group from our workshop going to a disco in Oak Bluffs.
Brown says, "Come on, you don't have to know anything"
when I say I don't know how. He says, "We'll have fun, come
be with us."

What I mean by not dancing is I only slow dance. I have
always watched Harold, who's a very good dancer, jitterbug
with other women while I sit the fast numbers out. But this
night it's disco dancing which Brown in his urging assured me
"You can't do wrong. Just get up in a dark corner and move to
the music by yourself."

And that's how it starts, that now I love to dance, that ten years later at Vermont College earning my MFA, others will see me leap to the floor as soon as I hear Aretha Franklin and figure I was always a dancer, the way my body goes toward the music.

This is my first night of *I go dancing*, I don't think of how I look, I hear the music, I get up and feel around for how its rhythms match me, move through me, and later, late at night, I know how to frame the poem I've started with my pine cone, a dangerous opening line: "The penis of my father grew." Though I'll have second thoughts and consider omitting it, I decide not to mess with its truth, to honor the line fearlessly, as if to honor my father. I am his future.

ON AN ISLAND

The penis of my father grew. On an island
after rain I walked to look for something
to bind me to this place and found a pine cone,
rain-soaked, soft brown; its petals curve
one over another into the tight bud of a boy.

Pine smell rises, deep New England pine.
I love the sticky resin oozing on my skin
and I would touch myself, but eyes,
two white spots on the stem like insect eyes,
catch me. The cone becomes a turd.

Becomes the uncircumcised cock of cossaks
who run the night in Byelorussia where my father
lived, the only son in a household so grand
there was a piano. He played. He wore spats.
But soon he will be hiding in a rain barrel

at the border. I have the foreskin of my father
to honor for America, to cherish for the Bronx,
to thank for Coney Island. I was there
and we were happy by the water. He brought me
my first bathing suit, white with bold red stripes.
I looked like a peppermint candy. He told me so.

One afternoon in the cellar of our bungalow
I saw him come out of the shower
I was coming down the stairs
(I'd been swimming in the bay)
I was coming down the stairs and I saw him. His penis.
I don't know what else. Only that
I saw a wonder.

What if a tick comes out of this cone
and sucks my blood? Still
I don't let go. Fear and all
I hold it in my palm. It flexes gently,
prickly, as I fold my fingers over
to make a nest, a solid hemisphere.

When I bring the poem to the workshop, Galway applauds.
I get the boyish beam. He speaks of its middle section as Whit-
manesque singing. The whole process is a turning point for me,
the way the poem came, the way it is received. And in these
extraordinary two weeks I am not the only one who changes.
I can still remember poems from that workshop, the leaps
people made. In a golden intensity we popped like corn.

One evening I run into Galway with his fourteen-year-old
son, Fergus. Fergus of Yeats' poems. Fergus of the Kinnell
poem that gave me harmony when I was so edgy. Fergus is visiting, and Galway, worried that he's sick, wants me to feel his
head for fever. I put the back of my hand to the forehead of

Fergus, then my cheek against his cheek to feel for heat as I do
with my own children. "He's fine," I say. Nurturer and poet,
my worlds are overlapping!

These amazing experiences, writing with my father as
muse, I'm sure I owe in part to Sharon Olds. The power of her
poems, her attention to the father, gives me permission. This
woman with her strong family poems encourages my ambition
as I struggle with fears of being a middle-aged dilettante. Even
in stupid ways I feel affirmed. When she's teaching the group
at the house where I'm staying and she asks, "Is there tea in
the kitchen?" I pour her a cup from the pot I've made, and
when she remarks on its quality, I take it as all-encompassing
admiration.

One afternoon Galway plays phonograph records of poets'
voices in order to talk about language. "Language is dying in
our mouths," he claims. He speaks of the attempt of American
poets to escape our uninflected drone. We listen to Ezra Pound
sounding like an Irishman; "the shmuck from Idaho turned
Yeats," Galway comments, and when a woman from our
group questions his deprecating remark, he talks about his own
voice as acquired: "I'm the shmuck from Rhode Island." It's
important for me to hear that this life we lead is a made thing,
that the poet creates him/herself.

Midway in the workshop Galway has arranged for a bar-
becue on the beach. I continue to see that here is a man who
teaches by building community. He himself scales and cuts fish
for the grill; after we eat he gathers us in a circle to recite poems
or sing songs we know by heart. In the center he's placed kin-
dling he picked up for the fire he will light.

When it's my turn to recite, I decide it might be fun to sing
My Yiddishe Mama; I don't know why. I ask the group if they
want Schmaltz or Yeats. "We've had Yeats," someone says,
"let's hear schmaltz." And I do it, sing with full voice a childhood song. I feel colorful. All the rest of the evening I keep

singing to myself and to the crescent moon and to the ocean in front of us and the pond in back.

Before I leave the Vineyard, I want to write a poem as a present for Harold, to say thank you from the fullness of my heart for the fullness of my two weeks. I go shopping and come away with a heart-shaped picture frame, thinking of the photographs he's always taking. I stare at the frame a long time, holding it to my cheek, fingering it.

I want to write something he'll like, something sincere like the solid brass of it. Heart-shaped, it's a cliché but that, too, feels real. I want to be an everyday lover. T. S. Eliot wouldn't buy it, but W. B. Yeats would surely include it in the fair and foul of love's mansion.

THIS HEART
for Harold

Yes I know I want what's real
so the seal stamped *solid brass*

fastened to the glass convinces
me to buy this picture frame

only a teenager would go for
or a lover with bad taste.

It's not easy being tacky, risking
a cliché to say I love you.

Poetry from such a place as
Have A Heart must be an urge

to have one, to say yes
to your polaroid and yes

to all the plastic of our clumsy lives,
yes to the hokum and the hooey

of a marriage neither young nor pure.
There's a porno thrill I get

in giving you this frame
in loving you with my eyes open.

On our last night, in an old, island house built across from the water, we're given a farewell dinner, after which we recite a poem we've memorized from the tradition of great ones. I've chosen early Yeats, "The Cap and Bells." I begin:

The jester walked in the garden:
The garden had fallen still;
He bade his soul rise upward
And stand on her window-sill.

Out the window I can see the water and the ferry moving across it. On it I will go home a good person. For days after, no matter what happens around me, I'll feel serene and alive, touched to tears by the slightest beauty.

Third Sublet

Gramercy Park, 1982–83

Returning to chattanooga from the Vineyard, from being truly at home, loved and loving, even Harold new to me and shining from the way we were together in Greece, I find my dreams insist on kicking me out of Eden.

Last night, as I slept, I stepped into a room filled with baby shit which came not from a newborn but a terminally ill woman in a hotel room. Everywhere I went I carried it on my feet. I was there as the graduation speaker at a women's college. As I began speaking, I noticed husbands and sons. I adjusted my words for them and said as much, wanting to recognize them too. But the speech became less real; I was a stranger trying for intimacy and profundity; the audience sensed it, their attention wandered, they began to move around and away from me.

Feeling alienated, I want the kinship of my poet friends. I'm eager to go to New York to look for another sublet. Harold is becoming a rube again; buying a TV is what he did yesterday, the better to watch the Jerry Lewis Labor Day telethon. I get a terrible headache and go to sleep.

I dream I'm at a festival with exhibits and lectures in tents. Harold is going to teach a class I'll audit as he's audited mine. Outside, talking to an old friend who's been ill, I go on and on about poets and poetry, encouraged by her interest. As we sit on a bench across from the Arts Guild, a big truck rounds the bend; I sense it's losing control, it's on the loose, turning over, then righting itself. As it comes toward us, I feel it may lose control again and run into me. Immediately I jump and race toward the field of tents, back from the traffic. Good thing. It crashes into my side of the bench. Later, the sick woman says how wonderful I knew to get up and move away.

I'm in New York, looking for a third sublet. This time it's harder to find. After several days I see an ad in the *Times* for a place in Gramercy Park. When I go to see the apartment, I find it faces heavy traffic on Third Avenue, and the decor is not appealing, but I'll be able to live in it. And I like the chance it will give me to try another Manhattan neighborhood. I return to Chattanooga satisfied that I'm set; come fall I know I'll be in the city.

Just before I leave for the sublet at the beginning of October, Harold's sister Becky is diagnosed with breast cancer. Her breast is removed.

Becky lives thirty miles away from us, in Dalton, Georgia, the town where Harold has his factory, the town where my father moved us when I was a child. Her husband works with Harold. As a young girl, Becky was a dancer though her father forbid her to dance professionally. She tried college, left, became a secretary, then married her childhood sweetheart. Our daughter, Judith, who dances, feels especially close to her.

I feel I walk away from Becky's illness when I fly to New York on October 3rd. Waiting in Gramercy Park, Tanya, the woman who owns the apartment, wants to talk. I'm there early to pick up the keys. Almost immediately she starts to tell me about her life, leaving her marriage, spending time in Jamaica, finally coming to herself. Tanya is bitter about her mother's wasted life. For twenty-five years her beautiful, petite French

mother was the kept woman of a married, wealthy, Orthodox
Jewish diamond merchant. Every day, she says, he came to fuck
her, ate his cottage cheese from its kosher container and went
home. They went out sometimes, she always walking behind.
They traveled to Europe, to Antwerp, always on separate days,
in separate rooms. Last year, Tanya tells me, the man died in a
hotel room the day after her mother left. Of course she couldn't
go to the funeral. Now she has nothing. Has Tanya told me this
story because I seem to have something? Because I'm coming for
fulfillment without a man? She wants to know about my life.
For hours we sit on the sofa facing Third Avenue, the strong sun
coming in from the east. She's not quite ready to walk away from
her apartment. When she leaves, I remain sitting on the sofa,
full of story and the Third Avenue sun, too dazed to get up and
explore the streets in my new neighborhood.

This is a stranger's house; that's my first feeling. When finally I look around, I see the apartment is decidedly divided
into light *and* dark. The sun never shines in the entry foyer, sep-
arated from the living room by a hanging of brown beads, nor
in the small, square kitchen off the entry, nor in the little hall
separating living room from bedroom, where the bathroom is.
The bedroom will be light in the morning, dim after noon. All
the fabric colors and beaded hangings are dull. The sunlight and
lamplight on Third Avenue and the curtainless windows facing
east keep the living room bright. That I'm on the sixth floor,
not lower, helps too. In the months ahead I will always make my
way to the front of the apartment and the sofas there

By late afternoon I'm eager to get out, explore a bit, find the
grocery, make myself part of New York again. Gramercy Park
feels like a downtown, noisier version of the Upper East Side
with people who are business types; yet the post-war, tall apartment buildings and stores on Third Avenue stand in contrast to
pockets of old charm nearby that remind me of the West Village
gone elite. Two blocks south the elegant Park requires a key for

entry; old houses surround it, the National Arts Club, an old Sanford White building, and lamplights, bringing to my mind residential squares in London.

In the evening I find a corner restaurant on Irving Place, one of the charming pockets west of my sublet. On the opposite corner is Pete's Tavern, an old pub where I'm told O'Henry wrote his stories. After my day with Tanya, I don't want old nor do I want sad stories. I choose the peaceful glamour of white cloths, white china, my very own tall, silver peppermill. Lace curtains cover only half the window near my table so I can look out at the street's glow. The waiter brings me a glass of crisp, white wine, a roll and butter. The promise of fish with dill. I sip as I stare at the beauty of the room, in its center a large, wooden table spread for the season with apples, cakes, and pies, and, beside a vase of orange lilies, an enormous, candle-lit pumpkin.

A man at the next table leans over to say, when his woman friend leaves for the bathroom, "I admire your eating alone, writing in your book." I sit up, bliss walking straight through me.

Galway Kinnell has been named director of a new writing program at New York University, and I hold in my mind his invitation to join the program. Since it is a graduate degree program I need to make advance preparations to enroll; I'll do that for the spring semester.

During this fall I've planned to work with both Jean Valentine and Sharon Olds at the 92nd Street Y; I applied and I've been accepted. I'm also taking an afternoon literature class at the New School taught by Gioia Timpanelli, a passionate storyteller and writer I met through Robert Bly.

After a few classes Valentine, who is very nurturing, tells me about a group of women who meet regularly to work on poems and suggests I send them my poems. I do and they take me into their poetry group. Seventeen years later we're still meeting, all of us having worked with Jean. We are a Valentine family.

Sharon Olds' class meets at the Y the night following Jean's; the contrast is perfect. With Sharon we are to focus only on new work, to build one poem on the back of the one before; I like that idea. Gioia's class at the New School is a treat, rich in her feeling for form.

Although I begin to realize my sister-in-law Becky is extremely ill, I don't dwell on it. I am glad to be in New York; no one back home has said death. But something old in me is stirring, maybe my mother's death, maybe the secret of her daughter Shirley's death which I discovered when I was eleven. Years later, in 1996, Jean Valentine will write a blurb for my first book of poems, and her wisdom will make me conscious of an unacknowledged truth: "[Myra's] profoundest education is death ... death and the life within it."

As I work on a new poem, "Topless Dancer in a Dressing Room," I see I'm dealing roundabout with Becky's breast cancer. When I read a rough draft to my friend Ingrid, she makes me aware of it. This year Ingrid lives only nine blocks from my sublet, Gramercy Park bordering as it does on the East Village. I met her four years before the first sublet, at a workshop I attended the summer after my mother died. I had just begun to write; she was in her early thirties, I, in my mid-forties. I think of her as my oldest writing friend.

The year my mother died, 1977, was when I began, steadily, to write poems. I don't know why I waited until her death to write. Or why, if death were the inspiration, I didn't write after my father died two years earlier. When she died, poem after poem came, along with the knowledge that writing would be my work for the rest of my life.

During the winter of '76-77, when my mother Ida (I want

to say her name) was seventy-five, she was diagnosed with colon cancer. At first she stayed with my sister, Raina, in Chicago, where we thought the doctors and care would be superior to what she'd get in Miami where she lived.

We were new to cancer information in the seventies; doctors rarely spoke openly about the disease, its effects or prognosis. All I remember is the doctor telling us immediately after Mama's surgery that maybe she would like being on the deluxe floor of the hospital where she could order lobster if she wanted it: "Give her whatever makes her happy," he said.

We didn't get it, that he was telling us she would die soon, that the operation didn't succeed in ridding her of the cancer. When she recovered from surgery, she flew back to Miami, and not long afterward she experienced abdominal pain again. We were surprised. I flew down to be with her when she went to see the Miami doctor recommended by the Chicago surgeon.

Dr. Glassman. His name is listed in the red faille address book my mother kept. It preserves her neat writing, nondescript compared to my father's practiced, elegant hand, his DMStein embroidered across the hem of the handkerchief I keep tucked between scarves in my drawer. Dr. Glassman told my mother she would have to undergo a second operation to perfect the first. Or did he say explore? Okay, we thought, he'd make it right and that would be that. He never mentioned terminal cancer.

Only after the operation, when my sister and I were waiting to hear, did he come to tell us the real news. The cancer had spread greatly, his interns and residents were amazed – oh, I thought, she was on display – and the only action now was to keep her as comfortable as possible, free from pain.

"She should be at home," we said when we recovered from the enormous shock. He agreed. She should die a dignified death, I said; we could give her that. What I meant by dignity was something I'd witnessed the summer before.

My cousin Sheli's mother-in-law had died of cancer, months

of dying, in their house on Shelter Island, NY, with her husband at her side and her children taking turns to visit. Sheli and her mother Sophie were always my models for rightness, and death was no exception. When it was ours to live through, I said we should take turns going to Florida and hire a local person as nurse-companion. My sister agreed.

For three months, at the beginning of 1977, we flew to Florida to be with Mama. It was not easy but it was not a sacrifice. I was able to keep my part-time teaching job. Getting away from home and traveling, racing off, suited me; it felt useful and loving.

I wish I could say I became closer to my mother through those months, but we were not any more intimate than before. Did she know she was dying? We didn't say so. We were as covert as the doctors and as we'd been through all the years of our lives. Her sense of privacy or beauty insisted we not allow any neighbors or friends to see her. We, of course, went along with her wishes, her old way of secrets.

Sometimes I'd leave her side to go to the grocery and out for lunch in the February/March tropical warmth. Leaving the close apartment, walking out into a landscape of lush palm trees and hibiscus, I felt as if I were repeating old escapes, my mother's, mine, relishing time away from children, and I'd feel guilty to see her look at me standing, going out. As if by having access to the door I'd triumphed.

Rarely in Miami together, my sister and I talked constantly on the telephone. Growing up, she was always Mama's favorite, the way one child will be easier or somehow more kindred. With Raina Mama shared a love of shopping and clothes and cooking and her secrets about men. I harbored the wish for my cousin Sophie to be my mother, someone outspoken, active, and intellectual, a modern woman who had ideas and stood up for them. With my own mother I didn't fit; I felt ugly and troublesome. The weekend she died, Raina was the one there.

I was supposed to be in Miami, but Raina had called us to come down the weekend before. She was uneasy; she was sure it was the end. Harold and I were about to leave for New York City to be with our daughter Karen for her twenty-first birthday. Karen was coming to the city from Bard College where she was in her senior year. When Raina called, scared, we postponed the celebration for a week and flew to Florida instead. Mama didn't die. It was good, all of us being together. Raina and Harold are very fond of each other, and Mama was glad, I think, to feel the presence of a man and one she loved.

Raina remained in Florida; we went back to Chattanooga, and five days later flew to New York for Karen's postponed birthday celebration. That's when Mama died. March 21st. We had returned from an evening of dinner and the musical *Chicago* (chosen because that's where Karen was born). About two in the morning, the telephone rang.

"Mama died," Raina sobbed, exhausted. "I went to her neighbors. They let me in, they helped me." I kept thinking she was the one there with Mama. I wanted it to be me, as it would have been if not for the postponed birthday celebration. I felt cheated. Yet the place where I found myself when Mama died was New York; all night until we caught the first plane to Miami I looked out at the buildings lit up all around and close to me; they held me. Death and birth. They come together so often in my life and make me crazy. Maybe it's because I carry the knowledge that if not for my sister Shirley's death I would never have been born.

Poems began to come one after the other when I returned to Chattanooga from Mama's funeral. I was almost forty-five, with no mother or father. This is how I'll grow old, I started thinking, I'll work with poems. And I began to take one day each week as a day of devotion to that thought. Wednesday. My Sabbath, I called it. On that day I stayed home and did not teach; I took no phone calls, ran no errands, gave myself to solitude, to read, to write until late in the afternoon when I picked up Judith from school or dance.

In April, a month after Mama died, I saw an ad in *Ms.* magazine for a woman's writing workshop sponsored by Hartwick College in Oneonta, New York. I can do that, I thought, bring my poems to a community of women. So in 1977, four years before the first sublet, I was on my way to my first writing workshop.

Getting there turned out to be momentous. From Chattanooga I had to change planes at LaGuardia in New York City to a small aircraft leaving from Butler Aviation nearby. Why go early to that tiny airport, I figured, when with my long layover I could go to the lounge upstairs in the main terminal, order a drink, sit near the window and write to a close friend in Israel the details of my mother's death. I looked at my watch, the blue Omega I still wear today, and saw I had plenty of time. I kept writing, sitting, staring out the window, until suddenly, glancing up at a wall clock, it was ten minutes past my departure. Surely a mistake. Then I knew my watch had stopped. Never before, never since.

By the time I got over to Butler Aviation, the plane was gone, the last flight of the day. "We paged you," the man at the counter kept repeating. "We can't fly after dark, and we were holding the flight as long as we could."

I had to make it happen, get myself to Oneonta. My first thought was to call Harold; I wanted to cry, to vent my anger, which is what I'd have done if he were with me. Then I reconsidered. "Do this alone, carry yourself," I thought. And the resolve to put one foot in front of the other calmed me. I made inquiries, went back to the main terminal at LaGuardia and found I needed to fly to Binghamton on a regular jet, then get a taxi to take me the forty miles to Oneonta. It would cost big bucks but I had to do it. And I did.

When the taxi pulled into the workshop site past midnight,

I found a few women awake, and someone led me to an empty
bunk where I plopped myself until morning. That's when I met
Ingrid who had an extra bed in her cabin, provided I didn't
smoke and would be quiet during her time to meditate. She
was as bossy as I am, as my cousin Sophie. She was a New
Yorker. I moved in.

Ingrid

Since I roomed with Ingrid in 1977 when my mother's death
was uppermost in my mind, she's become the one I talk to
about family once I'm in New York for the sublets. She's clear
that I must take charge of my life as a writer. With her I'm free
to say what I feel. She knows how much I need to be alone,
and how villainous I can be made to feel by my desires.

The first few weeks in my Gramercy Park sublet I'm still cop-
ing with its bizarre decor, the beaded hangings, the dark brown
bedspread in a room of somber Spanish-style furniture, and the
phone rings. The voice asks for Tanya. I explain, "Tanya isn't
in, she isn't in the city." Then my southern politeness, "But I'd
be glad to give her your message."

The quiet voice tells me, "Just say Doris called."

I've been sitting at the oak dining table. I spoon my soft-
boiled egg into a cup, and the phone rings again. It's Doris
whispering she isn't feeling good, asking how to take an enema.

"Well, I don't, I mean I haven't...," I'm sputtering. Yet a
woman is asking for my help. I summon reason: "Fill the bag
halfway with water. Warm. Maybe you could buy one fixed, a
Fleet" – reason's tricky – "oh, but you're afraid to go outside."

I eat the egg. It's cold. Truck brakes grind floors below.
When the phone rings again, Doris pleads, "If I come over,
would you give me an enema?"

I slam the receiver back on its cradle. I'm in tears. How did
I get myself into this state? Of course, by answering the phone
in the morning when I've made a practice of keeping those hours

to myself. But I'm not settled yet. Okay, this is what I get. And if I want to take it as a message for me in Tanya's apartment, her mother's helpless story still hanging in the air, I'd better start to work. The role of nurturer I must use on myself.

By the end of October I'm working on the new poem, "Topless Dancer in a Dressing Room," that has my heart, a poem domestic and muscular, a tough poem to write. I keep losing it. I decide to use it as a first poem in Sharon Olds' class, and when I do, I get strong, positive response and good help from my peers. They speak of the poem when we go out for drinks after class at the Old Town Bar, a raunchy place someone in the workshop suggests – no wine, only hard liquor– that turns out to be near my sublet. I order Jack Daniels on the rocks, a first, and under the spell of that evening return to the poem.

TOPLESS DANCER IN A DRESSING ROOM
(after a photograph by Diane Arbus)

All day she turns under sunlamps
to darken – except for breasts –
so when she's dressed
her breasts outshine
the feathered, sequined gown
designed to open on that whiteness.
Beautiful and calm
straight into the lens she stares:

> *Take me, come on*
> *take me –*

Her finger pushes
one white breast to make it shine out more.

I can't stop staring
at that frame, her breasts

so proud against the dark. My body
roars, bombarded by a drill: September
chilling leaves to new color, my daughter
off to Providence to begin her second year.
The door is closed on the flattened bed.

                                    I'm scared.

Sadness is turning into anger
turning breasts to fists. I want to break
from the clutter of a dressing room
and come out fighting.

I crack an egg
into warm, honeyed milk
and stir so there's no lump
stir until it's silk.

                    Come on, sweet cells, easy,
                    now don't gang up on me –

I pull the milk
through all my bones.
Still, I want a deeper sweet –
I lift the spoon, that sweet concave
from the honey jar, and lick it.

A strange thing, I realize. I have much more invested in my
younger daughter Judith's happiness than I imagined I would.
Somehow, through grammar school and high school, as a star
in her ballet and modern dance community, as an A student,
her successful, good place in the world I've taken for granted.
She was born in 1962 with the Women's Movement; she has that
advantage over Karen. Born six years earlier, Karen came before I had any awareness of how to make a life. Judith arrived
with the new world.

    When I began subletting in New York, Judith was a freshman in college and Karen had graduated with a degree in drama and was beginning her work and struggle as a stage manager in Los Angeles. Suddenly Judith began to struggle. That surprised me. After all, women now had support and consciousness, guidance unlike my ignorance when I went to the University of Texas and married at twenty, never having lived on my own. Could Judith go off in the wrong direction for years as I had? I guess what scared me was something primal – what if the mother has to die before the daughter really lives?! I am haunted by the fact that I didn't begin to write poems until my mother died and I don't know why I waited. Does loss, the absence of a mother, press us to mother ourselves, to give birth to our spirit as she gave birth to our body?

Judith calls me in New York. She wants to talk about her poor grade in art history: "I do the reading, I have great interest, I understand the lectures when others complain – why didn't I do better?" She's unhappy about a lot of things: where she's living, the woman she's chosen to room with, and now her classes. I don't question her about a social life with guys because that's not important, I think. I'm trying to turn patterns around.

I remember a dream I had when Karen seemed a mess, and I was at a loss to help her, the dream of Dove, an older woman with a round body, who wore an exquisite, embroidered belt. Standing by the bed, packing her suitcase for a trip, Dove told me, "Love her, just love her." I tried to let the peace of those words teach me that I didn't have to do more than love Karen. And now Judith. Just love her. The bond is there; let go.

Many of us cheer Nora as she closes the door at the end of *A Doll's House*, husband and children behind her. I feel lucky I found a way to leave without slamming the door, without losing my marriage and our family and the history built inside. Like Nora I wanted my own life. An apartment. It is a perfect word to describe the place I had to have, a place apart, a part

of New York City life where my light shines from a building
surrounded by other lights shining. They promise me life exists
within and outside of me, all of us a part of this world. Between my family house and my sublets is the threshold. In
stages I've learned how to open the door, how to walk out and
in, cross back and forth. From experiencing this threshold vis-
cerally, I arrive at "the possibility/ of entertaining beauty,/ doors
opening, you inside," lines I use in a poem.

It's bound to take time to undo over twenty years of moth-
ering others. Even with the enormous move I made, coming to
New York, habits and the mind don't automatically detach. By
this third sublet in late 1982, I've had both my daughters visit,
as well as relatives, friends, and my husband coming and going.
Something has to happen to me internally, with time, in the
smallest ways, to become the writer through and through.

Early on, when the children were young, there was no such
sense of threshold. By convention I was the one who stayed
home. Harold went off to his work each day, to his separate life
until seven o'clock or later each evening. My job, suitable or
not, was house work.

When Karen was three, we'd moved South from Chicago
for Harold to start his factory so I had my parents nearby for
help, and when Harold's business grew, I hired help. Judith was
born the week Karen entered first grade. We'd planned to have
a second child three years earlier, the children three years apart
according to some notion I had of "the right way," but my
body knew better. With the children six years apart, I could
tend them one at a time, and even that stretched me. I wanted
to read, to go to school, to be with ideas and adults. When at
last both children were school age, in addition to classes at the
university, I started working part-time in the reference room of
the Chattanooga Public Library. Student, librarian and, later,
teacher – those jobs suited me. But the job of mother, the one
who car pools, who goes to afterschool activities and takes in-

struction on costumes, endless attention to children, felt like slavery. Karen and Judith were great kids; I simply didn't like the job I had to do.

Then I happened on a family ritual I could give myself to whole-heartedly: travel. Each year I'd plan a trip for the four of us to take together. Planning months ahead, flying to where we'd never been, finding ourselves in places we'd explored on maps, feeling named streets come alive under our feet, entering a new world we would become part of, these trips were the happiest creations of our family life. Of course, this joy was no surprise to Harold. My desire for travel had surfaced years before, for our honeymoon.

In New York City I feel as though I don't have to travel to come to the energy of city streets. Walking with friends or by myself is a never-ending joy. After a particularly beautiful evening with my friend Francine, I find a way to write about it. The poem comes so effortlessly out of pleasure that I don't even think it's much of a poem, but it's all I have to bring to my workshop with Jean Valentine the night we meet in November before Thanksgiving. I wait until the end of class to read it to the group so it won't be subject to comments, "just for the fun of it," I say.

THE KNOWLEDGE THAT I HAVE EVERYTHING IN THE GARDEN

At 10:30 last night on 1st Avenue
a man in a black jacket
a tall man with a mustache
was picking out a cantaloupe.
O New York! You give me
63° and a whole moon

in November, pyramids of fruit
stacked up on the sidewalk

and my friend, I'm walking with
my arm around my friend,
coming from a play
that had 11 women talking with

a love for household lamps,
snakehandling, plastics
as an image of eternity, and, right here,
on your east side

a handsome man giving his nose
to the sweetness of a melon.

Only after I keep the poem around as an homage to New York and read it for special occasions, and people remember it, quoting "O New York!" do I value it enough to submit it for publication. *Columbia*, a journal published by the Graduate Writing Division of Columbia University, includes it in an issue featuring new voices in poetry. Often it's hard to know which poems other people will like; it's hard to trust the ones I don't labor over.

At the end of 1982, when the Y workshops with Valentine and Olds are over and the holidays are about to begin, Harold, Karen, Judith, and I plan to travel to Spain. Though I used to pour myself into months of reading toward each trip, I don't want to give it that time now; the event no longer has to fulfill so many desires.

As a family we're scattered: Harold down South, still working in his business as he has for over twenty years, closing the factory for an annual December holiday, Karen coming east from her work in theatre and film in California, Judith on vacation from Brown University in her junior year. It's the four of us traveling again after a few years of Karen's not joining us for the holiday. We'll bring in 1983 together in Madrid.

The night before we leave New York, I walk along Third Avenue with Karen to pick up treats for the apartment: holly from Gramercy Florist, cake from Pie in the Sky, and, for our breakfast before the flight, lox and bagels from Zooky's. I love carrying the paper cone of flowers and the cake box tied with red string, walking home through bustle and a dusk of soft lights, sharing my neighborhood with Karen. The holiday has begun.

The taxi that takes us to Iberia at JFK, even that ride, sends us off with joy. The driver is an old-timer. From where I sit in back he looks like a hefty Paul Newman; his voice holds a rough warmth, his speech a scruffy intelligence. The lights are beginning to come on, and we sit in quiet as we drive by water, past LaGuardia, the car racing on a side road, lights shining on Long Island Sound. This is the city I take with me, and when I return, it will be to this glow.

The great pleasure on the trip to Spain will be a new camaraderie I'll experience with my daughters. On our first day in Madrid we go to the Prado. Judith is taking an art history course, and I love her knowledge of light and space in Velasquez's paintings – what I really love is the mother guided by the daughter. Karen walks ahead. Even as a small child she'd insist on her independence: "You go the front, I go the back," she'd command, climbing the back steps to the kitchen of our apartment in Chicago. Today she returns to where Harold, Judith, and I are still standing in front of the Velazquez to tell us she's discovered something "really wild." She leads us to *The Garden of Earthly Delights*, Heironymus Bosch, new-found to her, and I'm thrilled to be led by her excitement.

Here, at the end of 1982, the year I have turned fifty, I am turning to my daughters as people I enjoy being with. They come toward me as strong, interesting individuals who want

me to see where they are. It's a new place we have created, the
children we gave birth to standing before us as creative adults.
Suddenly we're eye to eye.

For another couple of days we'll sail on that joy, and then
Spain will serve not only to gather but also to separate us. First,
Harold will get sick in Toledo. Karen, Judith, and I will take off
alone, walking from our parador into the center of the city,
closed and very quiet because it's Christmas Day. In a souvenir
shop open near St. Martin's Bridge, Judith wonders, "Maybe
the owners aren't observing the holiday because they were Jews
in another life, before the Inquisition?"

From that store, each of us buys a piece of pottery. As the
sun is setting, up up up we climb for almost a mile back to the
parador. Exhausted and exhilarated, we return to Harold who
is still sick to his stomach. He continues to feel weak next day
when we drive to Seville. It's Sunday, again we're in a closed
city, so Karen, Judith, and I take a late morning walk to see
what we can see. Spain has felt like a masculine country to me
(maybe I'm tying gender to religion, thinking Inquisition, or
maybe it's Ernest Hemingway's novels and bullfights) so when
we stop to eat lunch in a local restaurant, it feels like a special
adventure, three women together who are strong and sophisticated, at ease and happy.

After checking on Harold who wants to keep sleeping, we
go out again to walk to the river, and find a promenade full of
people, our first lively street crowds since we arrived in Spain.
People are strolling and visiting on benches, many children and
families. I notice especially the young teenage girls in bright lip-
stick, dressed to be grown-up, getting ready for catching a man.
And the older teenagers with their young men, how they stroke
the man, how they sit with their bodies thrust forward towards
him, giving, giving. Bait. To catch, to have. I can remember the
time of those body movements and those wishes, to be with
a man, to be a couple, how it was my prime concern. Here

it's like being pushed back in time, before the Women's Movement, before the pleasure of three women happy together regardless of men. Of course, no sooner do I think this than I see Karen flirting with some Italian men in a cafe where we've stopped for coffee.

I look at us: Karen, who has become such an attractive woman, a woman with energy (as always) and strength (newly centered) and Judith who is struggling to gain her place out of childhood. During the early years of motherhood, of constant giving and the lack of solitude, I felt lost, but today I'm content. Though I still find myself too involved with family, a conditioning so deep it seems genetic, the source of power, I can respond with consciousness.

Then, by our second night in Seville, I'm the one sick, joining Harold in fading from the scene. Karen and Judith are on their own, planning their separate evening. I feel the future in that event, but it's okay. Sapped, I'm able to watch them go off, with expectations of enjoying news of their evening when they return. They are going to see a performance of flamenco. There's no way to know – amazing – that one day Judith will become a flamenco dancer/teacher.

Next day, in Cordova, still sick, we lie low. Karen is out, and we manage to join her in the late afternoon in the Plaza of Maimonedes. As we look for the statue of this doctor/teacher/ writer from Spain's golden age, before the Inquisition, we notice a swastika on a wall, and, finding the statue, we see another swastika on its base.

This was the old Jewish quarter, and there's supposed to be a synagogue here, which turns out to be a small one-room building. In its courtyard, off to the side, a man comes out asking for *dinero*. When Harold hands him some money, he lifts the latch on the door, and we enter a bare room. We take a few minutes to look – maybe there's something not apparent, but no, it's empty – and when we leave, the man comes out of his house with postcards. Harold asks, "Are you Jewish?" "No," he replies emphatically – "Catholic, Romana!"

Harold is the son of a rabbi, generations of rabbis. In Sophie's Marxist house, I grew up hearing *religion is the opiate of the people*. Searching for the home of Maimonedes, once more I'm aware of the way religion has been used to pit people against each other, to create wars and exert power. Maybe that's how human nature goes when men and women are so separate: women's power through giving birth, men's through gaining turf.

In our rented car Karen drives us south through Andalusia. By the time we arrive in Granada we've recovered from our stomach upsets, and together we warm to the sensuality of the Alhambra, to the feminine quality of its cuniescript, the gardens coming toward and around rooms, the fountains, the curve of every shape: pillars, arches, domes, and rippling water.

It's winter term again, two years since the January I came to the city to begin to make my way in a community of poets, at the New School and at the 92nd Street Y. This semester I'm a student in Galway Kinnell's graduate writing program at New York University. Frannie, from the Martha's Vineyard workshop, and Amy, from my first class at the New School, are in the program too, the new family I'm creating. Because Galway is so good at making community, those of us working with him are soon close-knit. His instruction to go to Eddie's after workshop, down the street from our class to continue talk of poems, will become a ritual we follow. Often he'll join us. Then we'll start seeing each other at readings in the city, arranging to meet, building support for each other and our poems.

My old family, husband and daughters I've just traveled with, are also making steady appearances in the city this winter. The more solidly separate I feel – and these sublets have

allowed me that strength – the less threatening others become.
I can welcome them, their love and good company. I can see
who they are. Judith has come in from Providence to spend the
weekend, and the weekend is over. Harold will come up on Friday night. In between I'm deliciously alone. I've come to feel
like a warm shore visited by waves. They leave and I know
they're coming back.

    As this rhythm continues, something new happens within
me, substantiating my freedom even as they visit, and it's not
the old distancing, keeping others at bay while I pretend to be
present. This shift hasn't occurred as a sudden miracle.
Through messages my body's given me, dreams and little ill-
nesses, I've created situations that insist I pay attention. During Judith's visit I needed to stay in with a cold, and she
managed to have a very nice weekend. When she left, I felt
good to think she didn't need me to provide her agenda, nor
did I feel guilty for absenting myself. It was a sensation that
extended the pleasure I'd felt in Spain, the sense of more instead of less, what she brought toward me from her separate
life, our two-ness.

    The days that followed her visit I took to hibernate in my
warm apartment, not caring about outside, finally trusting to its
being there for me, my city when I want it. At night, able to remain inside and quiet, I sat snugly in the corner of the sofa,
propped against a cushion, looking out at a darkness always lit
by other apartments, my books and papers collected around me.

    When Harold arrives, my cold is better, the laryngitis gone,
but I'm still feeling quiet. I'm thinking Harold will enjoy a Sam
Shepard play, *True West*, I'd seen earlier in the month; he could
go, I'd stay in on Saturday night. He's had a busy week so he's
glad for a leisurely Saturday morning, and in the afternoon,
after we take a walk, he decides to nap. I read. Lovely.

    When he wakes up, I ask what he wants to do. I've already
mentioned *True West* as a play he'd want to see, especially since

it's about two unlike brothers (which reminds me of his brother and him). It's very theatrical, a physical experience, a power struggle he's lived. But he doesn't say anything about wanting to go; we sit together, work on a crossword puzzle, nice and easy.

I ask again. It's getting too late to eat and then go to the play. He says he doesn't care; he'd rather hang around with me, just have dinner wherever, so I go into my planning mode. I mention Sal Anthony – it's just around the corner, good Italian food Harold can't get in Chattanooga. "Fine," he says. Then I think of a new place, Mon Paris on 30th Street. It would be fun to try someplace new, and French food doesn't exist in Chattanooga either. Harold says, "Let's call," which he does and then goes into the bedroom to change.

And I, washing up a few dishes in the kitchen, start to get nervous, not wanting the dinner I've arranged. I'd wanted Harold to say he was going out, I wanted to stay home for the evening with Harold returning later, full of his own news. Is this how I get sucked into a situation I plan and show up for, only to drift away from it, disconnected? Is this the origin of my dis-ease, wanting someone else to recognize or create what I want, my apartness?

Last night I promised myself, when I couldn't sleep in the middle of the night and feared I might relapse into illness, that the next day I'd go out only a bit. I would listen to my body and attend to its messages, if in turn it would keep me well. When I woke I did feel better. During the day, being quiet was just right. And tonight, though I don't feel bad, I'm suddenly anxious, realizing I don't want the French restaurant. I need to be alone for a few hours.

I walk into the bedroom and tell Harold all this, and he hears me! He says I should stay in and he'll go to the theatre. I breathe a deep breath. What a wild feeling! For a moment it's even frightening. As if I'd let go of Harold. As if I were suddenly to be left hanging in space.

When he leaves I'm enveloped by a great comfort. A length of quiet. I have the stretch of it. And Harold's coming back. Then I'll be animated by his story. I sit for a while looking out of the window, feeling the distant noises and all the other rooms of light in the darkness as a softness tumbling toward me into which I tunnel. I'm amazed by the gift of these days and what it's brought me to. But I don't want to fill this lovely time with words. I simply relish it.

The spring of 1983 I sometimes recall as the story of the soup. I could also call it my sister-in-law dying. It was to be our last Passover together, she and I laughing as we counted and mis-counted how many matzo balls we'd need for the Passover seder. But the story of the soup really begins earlier and has to do with my marriage. It started with a chicken. On my first trip back to Chattanooga after our December holiday in Spain and the harmonious New York City weekend in January with Harold, I decided I'd cook dinner for us, veal chops, because they'd been in the freezer a long time. This weekend I could take time to prepare them nicely. Though I like to eat, I don't like to cook, unless I'm in the kitchen with others. When I'm depressed I don't want to do it at all.

We were eating breakfast and Harold suddenly announced, "There's one thing I'd go out for today." I knew he had hours of work ahead of him; salesmen from all over the country were coming in the next day, and he had to prepare his speeches and organize the agenda for the intense week to follow.

It was a beautiful day. I'd wished for rain, for staying in, reading, writing, cooking while Harold worked. It felt like spring, Harold said, when he walked out to the driveway for the paper, so when he mentioned taking time away for one thing, I thought he couldn't resist the warm day and might be tempted to take a walk around the neighborhood.

"Chicken," he said. "I'd go out to get chicken for a chicken soup."

That seemed nice, having him express a desire, and as it happened, I too felt like having chicken soup. And a noodle pudding, I thought, to go with the soup; I'd make my mother's kugel. Back to the freezer went the veal chops. Mmmm, a delicious, homey meal. I told Harold I'd go to the grocery, no point in his taking time when it wouldn't even get him out to enjoy the pretty day. We talked for a while. I asked questions about the new printing press in his factory, and, in speaking, he seemed to get ideas for the next day. It was an interesting conversation.

As I drove to the grocery, I decided to go to Warner Park to walk around a bit, then stop by the bookstore to pick up a Sunday *New York Times*. The streets were deserted; in the bookstore I browsed and was excited to see the *Book Review* had a review of *The Death of an American*, which was written by our nephew, Becky's son David; it would be such a boost for Becky and Morris. Then I went to the Red Food Store for the chicken.

Home, chattering about what I'd done, I said I knew I'd been gone longer than I'd planned, but since I bought only half a chicken it wouldn't take long to clean it and get the soup started. "This won't make a big soup, but so what, we'll have plenty."

Then Harold replied, "You're always stingy, you always buy too little."

I was hurt, annoyed at his grouchy response. He closed the door between the dining room where he was working at the table, and the kitchen where I got busy, running water to wash the chicken and vegetables. I should let him know we're equals, I thought, we should be grateful to each other for things done. I felt taken for granted, that I'd offered to serve him something good and he wasn't glad for it.

Just as I finish putting up the soup and getting the noodle

mixture together, Harold comes into the kitchen. "It smells good," he says.

"I'm making a noodle pudding, too," I add, and he responds, "You always make the same thing, never something new."

That's it! He gets my speech on joylessness, on not being grateful, on his work valued more than mine. The back and forth begins.

"You're the one who always complains," he insists.

"For instance, when?" I push, insisting he come up with examples.

"Guacamole," he says, how I make him feel guilty for ordering chili and instead talk him into guacamole.

"That's not the same," I counter, "that's not giving something and being put down."

And he explodes, "If you're making the chicken soup as a gift for me, forget it. I don't need your gifts."

Though I go on to tell him I'm being misunderstood, that I want the soup too, that I'm making it for both of us, he walks out of the kitchen, "I'm not eating the soup or the pudding," and he goes back to work. Ultimatums. I'm stunned.

Two hours later when it's near done, I ask how long before he'll be ready to stop for dinner.

"I'm not eating your soup or pudding, I told you," he answers through the door. So I take what I want and sit down to eat at the kitchen table. It's delicious. Am I angry? Somehow I don't let it surface. I find pleasure in eating the good food, slowly, quietly. A bit later I make an ice cream soda for dessert. I open mail and write a letter and spend the evening productively. I pretend I'm alone, and my solitude feels good. Food, books, writing: my pleasures.

When Harold finishes his work, I try to avoid him to keep myself in my satisfied state. I go into the living room to read. After he takes something to eat – I don't know what, only that the refrigerator opens, dishes clatter, and later I see it's not soup or pudding – he decides to pay bills. After he's eaten, when I come back into the kitchen, I close the door to the dining room where he sits with the checkbook.

"Why are you closing the door?" he asks.

"I like it that way," I answer.

I'd begun therapy in New York in the fall, shortly after I took the Gramercy Park sublet. Therapy in Chattanooga in the mid-sixties and early seventies had supported me through the confusion of marriage and making an individual life. It combined with the Women's Movement, enabling awareness and the strength to act. I'd called it giving me a life. And when my mother died in 1977, I went back to that good therapist who suggested we see each other six times to make my way from her death. With a therapist in New York perhaps I wanted to deepen my experiences of freedom. At first I didn't realize I was also dealing with death, triggered by what was happening to Becky.

My friend Rosalind found me the New York therapist – Gloria. As soon as I heard her name I said Yes. The first poem I wrote after coming to New York used her name to address the city; I chose it for its exuberance and because it was the name I'd wanted to be called as a child, what I'd named my favorite doll. Gloria as therapist felt like destiny.

After the incident of the soup, when I return to New York, I know I'll have the support of Gloria. Additional strength comes from the bi-monthly meetings with the poetry group Jean Valentine suggested I join. We do not bring our personal lives to each other to sit around and discuss; we bring new poems to hear out loud and make stronger. When intimacies surface, they are revealed and understood through what we write. In that deep way, month after month, by now year after year, we've become a poet-family.

Since we meet in each other's homes, I invite the group to

the Gramercy Park sublet. I'm just back from Chattanooga with a poem that tries to get at my anger with Harold. It's called "The Fit," and after I read it, as usual someone in the group volunteers to read the poem back to me. That's when I hear the doubleness of the word "fit," how perfectly it satisfies both the old tantrums and new desire to find my place.

THE FIT

He'd left me,
not saying that he'd left me,
not gone, but
         the fit
that comes from every absence
that is present, from the person
who unclicks you in his head,
                  who says
he's in your life but isn't
there, like a curb within a dream
you put your foot down from and suddenly
                       no landing
you're falling, the step is air.
All the business of the dresser
I shoved off: papers, paper clips,
                my museum
calendar, tickets to *Les Miz*, tickets
for a flight to Chattanooga
cluttered the carpet to the bed: the thousand proofs
                      we live
getting somewhere, always
planning, arriving – then the vanishing
as if the other is too much to bear.
                Dirty clothes
stuffed in the hamper

I pulled out, and this time sorted
not to do a wash but just to

                              erect mountains:
slips, bras, pantihose,
socks, undershorts, and shirts. Evidence –
that's not it but what is felt by it when

                                        it couples

with a word like *hard* – hard
evidence I needed underneath my feet.
I had to step on piles of it to sleep.

The next time I'm in Chattanooga, Harold's brother, Charles, comes to visit with his new wife. She's thirty-two years old, and I resent having to entertain them. He's three years older than Harold, very handsome and creative and the rebel of the family. He ran away from his first wife, just took off and left her. She was a nurse from Louisiana he'd married during the Second World War when, underage, he'd run away to join the coast guard; he was wounded and she nursed him. They never had children, which, according to doctors, was his problem. After he left her and resurfaced out west, he married a Mississippi woman he'd met there, a teacher with whom over the next ten years he had four children. Now, in 1983, there's a nice, young Memphis woman who works for the juvenile court to take care of him and his family. She's the new wife Charles is bringing to visit. I'm angry about the women he's stepped over to get to this one, angry about how they've been erased, how they sank and he endures, angry at their lack of strength and also frightened by it.

Yet I came back to Chattanooga to be with Harold, Charles, and Linda. And I act like a witch, the sour hostess, while Harold becomes the magnanimous host. Before Charles arrived, I'd had a night with Harold when I couldn't stop screaming: about the soup, about Charles. I'd let myself scream until, dizzy and cold, my head felt light. I know I scared Harold. He expressed his pain at seeing me so distraught but I had to scream.

Last December, in my conference with Sharon Olds, toward the end of her workshop, she told me, "Get at the violence. It's the other side of wonder in you." And she gave me an image for how it should work: a runner in a race never stops at the finish line, never right on it; he always runs beyond. I remember being excited by that power, instructed to use what I knew to be mine, a desire to switch on every light, a hunger to eat everything on my plate. Like being told years ago by Steve Orlen at Bread Loaf that I was a good writer, but I needed to study with poets to strengthen my natural gift, his giving me the word *Go*, the command you wait for at the start of a run. And with that permission I ran to New York.

When Sharon tried to explain violence, she made me think of what we usually characterize as *witch*. Soon afterward I heard Gioia Timpanelli tell an old Irish folktale about King Arthur's knight Gawain who needs to find the answer to the question *what do women want most*? Dame Ragnell, a noble beauty under a spell that has turned her into a witch, knows the answer; she will reveal it to him if he marries her, witch and all. When she tells him what women want most is *sovereignty* and Gawain honors it, she is transformed, all is happily ever after.

In New York I'd had nights of not sleeping, but I relished the stillness, the strength of needing no one, of being awake to thoughts, words that had shape to hold me solid in the darkness. I wanted to be at peace with my life, and at peace with marriage which is a big part of my life. Now in Galway's class I'm working on a new poem that tries to order the old struggle:

I wanted out. I wanted streets
but most of all I wanted
a dusk of unfamiliar people

where every life seemed possible.
As from a book. To be anonymous.
Men I didn't know took shape

every class I took: on the white tile
of a lab, down the aisle
of a mezzanine. Off the curb

at Michigan or Vine, lights
going come on, come on,
Go, my hair began to sway

from its barrette. But I didn't fall,
I climbed. At the teacher's feet
I took on Emma Bovary, a mother

I had to know. Pound and Eliot
played hard to get, rebuffed me
so I felt dirtied, sometimes

desperate, but tough. I went places
through those books, and reached a center
that stayed put, even through a war.

Harold's sister Becky is dying. Becky, skeletal, in her cream silk
slacks with matching sweater and pearls. It's March – always
the month my mother dies – six years now since her death –
and, back from time in Chattanooga, I go to see my therapist,
Gloria, after which I shop, reach to pay for pearl earrings, and
my wallet's gone. Mentally I retrace my steps: the number 10
bus when I took out quarters for my fare, choosing the seat
next to someone in a big camel's hair coat, moving close to him
because the seat on the other side was dirty. At 72nd Street I re-

member an eerie sensation as I looked up to see the side of the Dakota Apartments, thinking *here I am, at the Dakota where John Lennon was shot.*

Did the robber steal my wallet at that moment? I didn't feel it happen. I don't know when a hand suddenly reached inside my purse. What if I die like that, one minute alive and a truck I don't see rams into me, gone off the face of this earth without a second of awareness?! The earrings were meant to replace good ones I'd lost. The store was sleazy. The woman waiting for her money reprimanded me, "You should have zipped your bag more carefully."

Kaput, the wallet gone. I'll start fresh, I think. New wallet. New IDs: Visa, driver's license, library card. New pictures. Start fresh? The city has given me the life I want, but there's no escaping loss. I walk home and keep myself going by reading the street signs: *Ambesol kills mouth pain on contact.*

I go back to Chattanooga for Passover. We sit around the table at Morris and Becky's house, gathered for our seder. Before the gefilte fish, before the soup with matzo balls, Becky stands to usher in the story of the exodus from Egypt. Until this night the men have always begun the service. We are all aware of Becky's choosing to stand because she has never done so before, and we know she'll never do it again. "Oh shit," she mutters as her voice breaks on the blessing.

Hours later, through the window near our bed, I keep looking at the moon since I cannot sleep. I feel my mouth open on its fullness as it fades. When I do fall asleep I dream I'm in bed with the comic playwright, Neil Simon, wanting to kiss him. Awake, disgusted, I question why I'm trying to make out with a writer of such insignificance to me, one whose work, in daylight, I don't like! I don't know the answer. In the dream no such question. Maybe the only point is loving the writer. Or accepting that I don't know why I've chosen the man I'm with. Or laughing at what fools we mortals be.

The morning I go back to New York after Passover, Harold and I wake out of two dreams. He says, "I dreamed of the most beautiful butterfly. I was inside, it was raining, and I said, 'See, you have to stay here safe, underneath the eaves,' and just then an enormous butterfly appeared and spread its wings, huge, beautiful, navy blue at the edges with circles of fuschia. I kept wanting to look at it, to own it, so I put it in a bottle. I knew it had to have a cap with holes for air which I was looking for when I woke. I was going to let it go eventually."

I say, " I dreamed my mother was going to jail. Lawyers had thought it best to determine she was guilty, and when she came back to town she was incarcerated. Ashamed, she was crying, hiding in a dark room behind a screen, and I was trying to get to her."

After a moment's thought, I say, "Our dreams fit. They're opposites that dovetail."

"Yes," Harold says.

When I arrive in New York, the apartment holds its rooms out to me, and I am very happy to walk away from prison and death into them.

It's balmy spring in the city. Pear trees are in bloom; white blossoms line 9th Street. I'm ambling toward the university, and I see Galway Kinnell, there on Waverly. When I was in Chattanooga I read that he'd won an American Book Award so I say "Congratulations."

"How did you know?" he beams, "I've just heard."

And when I tell him I saw it in the paper a few days ago, he says, " Oh yes, the American Book Award, thank you, but just now, this hour, I received a call. I've been given the Pulitzer Prize."

Oh! Oh! I'm too excited to repeat congratulations. We simply stand there amazed, awkward, shy, overcome by such news. I'm the first person he's seen since the call. He probably wouldn't have spoken if I hadn't come toward him with greetings. And when we part – "See you in class" – I don't know how to contain myself. Should I tell everyone in Washington Square Park, should I call someone?

By now Galway as well as those of us in the workshop are part of each other's world. Once he brought us a long poem he was working on, to take home for our comments. It was a marvelous exercise, welcoming us into his process and revision, witnessing rawness in a poem, even one written by a master. That poem will appear in the *New Yorker*, and we'll reap *naches* (that's Jewish for being proud). The new family. Years later, with money I've earned from a reading, I'll buy Galway's poem, "The Sekonk Woods," when I happen on it in a bookstore, a small press edition, the poem we saw in process published as a book with Lotte Jacobi photographs.

Walking into our workshop, I announce Galway's prize. Everyone wants to talk about it, but Galway says, "No, not now, we'll go to Eddie's to celebrate after class."

He says, "Let's get to the poems you've brought tonight. Who's memorized poems from the tradition to recite for us?"

I don't remember if we hear Amy recite Keats, or Frannie, Yeats, or me, Dickinson. But we go on with class as usual, listening to a few poems spoken by heart, after which we read our own poems for comments from our peers and Galway.

After class he comes to Eddie's as he promised; he celebrates the night of his prize with us as if, once more, to say we're all in this together. I rise to the occasion by buying the wine for everyone. This gesture feels like the generosity of an adult who is out in the world, not one a woman of my generation has been raised to – like a father or a husband who says "I'm paying, the drinks are on me." I think of Becky unaccustomed to rising to say the blessing at the seder, how she broke down. When the wine comes and I stand to make the toast to Galway, I feel regal and strong with love.

We stay at Eddie's a long time; Galway doesn't excuse himself early. Years later he speaks of these years in the NYU program as special, and all of us feel it, the history/the family we made then. It was as Judith Sherwin had told me two years before – my life would be formed with my poetry peers. Galway's gift for teaching, his love for poems has entered our way of making them. In the *New York Times* the next day the announcement of the Pulitzer Prizes appears, with the poetry award to Galway Kinnell for *Selected Poems*. "The book ranges from pastoral odes to the sounds of New York City."

It is the night of my debut, the first public performance of my poems. When a man from a small publishing house called my sublet in March, asking me to take part in the reading series he was organizing the following month, I said Yes immediately. Nervous or not I knew this was an opportunity, a next step.

My name had been given to the publisher by Shelley Mason, director of the 92nd Street Y Poetry Center. She and I have stayed in touch ever since I first walked into her office, new to the city, wide-eyed and questioning. She'll come to hear my poems.

Yes, I'd said like a professional. So now I'll act like one. I will be one of six readers of poetry and fiction; I sense I must do something that will give a shape to the reading. I look at the poems I've written these past two and a half years in New York.

I become less nervous; somehow I separate myself from the poems; they stand apart as good fortune, as work I must trust. I tell myself to honor them that way. What I can do is present them right, and I decide to connect them to the occasion, the place and people; I order them into a kind of narrative of a woman who's come to this city.

To present myself I choose a long peasant skirt, an Indian design with slate blue stripes ending in geometric shapes of red, green, and blue. On my feet soft, black leather boots. It's a Russian look when I add a tunic, a white cotton overblouse, and, since it's still cool these spring evenings, I put on the heather green wool sweater with wooden buttons Sophie knit last year for my fiftieth birthday. It's just right, I can tell, and later, friends say so, that I look poetic, part of the East Village.

The poems have been made; that work is done. I revised as I practiced because hearing poems out loud makes a big difference. Now they're on their own. It's like being a parent, the way I feel the poems are mine and not mine.

My old friend Francine, my first sharer of fantasies, is coming with two southern friends of hers. For Francine it's still men that bring us new worlds, but we continue to share enthusiastic natures. And our history. I'll read a poem I wrote when she and her friends, also up from Tennessee, came down to my sublet in the Village, when "poems blew like wheat, waiting/ for a harvest."

We're meeting for dinner at Pier Nine, a restaurant in the East Village, after which we'll walk to St. Marks Place where the reading will take place in the basement of a Polish church.

An old friend from Chattanooga, Bill S., visiting the city this week, comes up behind me and puts his hands over my eyes as we stand outside the church. Guess who, and I do. More excitement when another person from my other life shows up, a former student of mine from an English class I taught at Notre Dame High School in Chattanooga.

At the church we discover the door hasn't been unlocked; we'll have to perform in the schoolroom across the street, with the audience on kindergarten chairs. It is a fitting introduction to the unpredictable world of poetry performance. Later I will hear Galway say a poet's responsibility is to the poems; the poet shows up and gives the reading for two people or hun-

dreds, in a basement or the Library of Congress. And that's
how it's been; by now I've read the range.

I'm ready. The publisher has placed my reading third, right
in the middle, just before the break for the next set. Perfect.
When I stand I begin with "Gloria, I'm Here in Your City" and
discover I know my poems by heart. I don't have to look down
at the pages. I am back in their world and the words walk out
of me. I hear laughter, sighs; I look at faces shining towards
me. Everyone is paying attention. I am comfortable and calm,
as if the excitement I felt earlier existed in another person.

When I finish there's a roar of applause. It's intermission,
and Ingrid rushes toward me with roses, Rosalind and Linda
with tears, Francine effusive with praise – "This is the real
you!" Bill and my student Gail and my workshop peers look
proud. It's a glorious sensation!

Toward the end of May, Harold comes for the weekend to
celebrate my fifty-first birthday, and the night he arrives I invite
my new poet-friend Frannie and her husband to join us. I like
the idea of beginning to build friendships with couples, to encourage a social life for the two of us here. As we talk over dinner, Frannie tells us she will visit her first husband's grave next
day, "for the first time since his death." We hear that he was
a journalist killed in Vietnam on May 21st. "That's my birthday," I say.

The next week it's time to give up my sublet. But a few days
before I leave, I go to a spring party for Friends of Poets &
Writers on the fiftieth floor of an apartment house on 57th
Street. I get myself to the windows: west the Hudson River
where the sun is about to set on New Jersey, south the excla-
mation points of World Trade at the city's tip, east the slant of
Citicorp and its new neighbor IBM shaped by Phillip Johnson
to resemble a Chippendale highboy in air. When I turn to the

room, Galway's there – "Hi Myra" – and Norman Mailer is
about to walk into me on his way to the hors d'oeuvres table.
I see poets from past workshops; we kiss and hug.

I eavesdrop on a conversation between the fiction writer,
Norma Klein, and a volunteer. "I'm an ardent theater-goer,"
says the young woman, "and I'm dying to see Caryl Churchill's
Cloud-9, but I can't seem to get downtown." I have to laugh
because from where we stand it takes fifteen minutes by subway. By now I'm aware of how New Yorkers consign themselves to neighborhoods, and downtown, where I live, is an
exotic world away from here. High on one glass of wine, I float
down to the street, down into the subway at Columbus Circle
where I catch the number 3 express to Brooklyn. I'm going to
have dinner with Brown, my Martha's Vineyard traveling pal.

The woman sitting next to me on the subway is reading a
book by Norma Klein, the author I was just standing beside at
the cheese table. I take out my journal to note the pleasure of
this, and when I look up, holding on to the strap in front of me,
a lovely-looking, gray-haired woman is smiling as if to say I
know what you're doing. When she gets a seat, she takes out
her notebook and begins to write. Only in New York!

Summer 1983

Tennessee, New York City,
Georgia, and Napa

WHEN I GIVE UP the Gramercy Park apartment to go back to Chattanooga for the summer, I no longer fear the hook will keep me there. Now I know the door will always be ajar.

Nonetheless, Chattanooga makes me crazy: the still green of lawns, no people on the streets near our house in any direction, only trees, shrubs, grass, houses, cars, as if people had been wiped out. When nothing stirs I start fights with Harold to move the air.

There is no one I see to whom poetry is central. When friends from Nashville come to visit with their baby, Harry does ask about my work. He and I met at the end of the sixties during the Vietnam War era when we taught together at a high school for emotionally disturbed adolescents. By leaving the University of California at Berkeley where he was a graduate student in history to teach at the high school, he took a stand against participating in the war. He was a kindred soul I was glad to work near; we loved each other's intelligence and energy. When I tell him about my sublet in New York this past year, how it ended with my reading with five others in the East Village, he says, "Are they still doing that, reading in coffee houses?" Meaning shades of the sixties. Meaning adolescence. Suddenly I feel insignificant, foolish, and unreal.

Desire In *The Marriage of Heaven and Hell,* William Blake writes, "Being restrained by degrees, [desire] becomes passive til it is only the shadow of desire." People around me here are disappearing on themselves long before they die.

Before Becky's cancer confines her to the house, we make a Sunday excursion to Reflection Riding, the nature preserve below Lookout Mountain. She and Morris have come from Dalton to Chattanooga for brunch after which we'll go to see wildflowers in bloom, the pond with ducks, the pasture with horses. To the right of the exit there's a shelter for wounded birds and animals. A hawk with one wing gone claws a branch and stares straight at us. Becky shivers, she cannot stay, we must walk away fast.

Watching Becky's fear, I think of being buried with insects under the earth. I remember as a schoolgirl fastening on William Cullen Bryant's poem, "Thanatopsis," wanting to read its romantic verses to my mother: "approach thy grave,/ Like one who wraps the drapery of his couch/ About him, and lies down to pleasant dreams." I wanted to make nice with death, perhaps to console my mother for the loss of her first child or for her own death.

Recently I read an article by Diana Trilling, a memory piece about a childhood marked by fear. Fear of lice. Having been isolated as a child, sent home from school after an inspection of my platinum blond hair, I understood the horror of such an invasion. Animals were making a home in me, and I must have sensed that ultimately, of course, there was no door.

The terror in Becky's face is calling me to new attention; when I get home I look again at "Thanatopsis": "Earth, that nourished thee, shall claim/ Thy growth ... to mix forever with the elements." I have time I tell myself. And let it be in the city! It may be foolish but I feel safer beside human nature than in wilderness.

We drive up the mountain to visit a couple whose house I've

wanted to see, their bedroom placed where a living room had been so that it can open to a porch and a cultivated garden of stones and flowers. Their bed is covered in soft, flowered cotton, a loose comforter, with many pillows scattered at one end. On one side sits a small floorlamp with a shade of painted birds. Tears well up in my eyes. Tamed nature, beauty and order. I cry as I did the first time I walked along the quays in Paris. I cry because we're all going to die, and we try so hard to cover up. Concreteness: it's what the city and my writing give me. Death always within us, we build to insist on life, an urgency that's poignant.

At the end of June Becky confronts Morris: "I know I'm dying. Why don't I get it over with; how do I die?" Harold and I drive down to Dalton from Chattanooga to be with her and Morris and their son David who's flown in from Utah. I sit with Becky, but she isn't going to say anything to me, and I don't know what to say to her. My intelligence, my experience, everything goes limp and sour as I lean to kiss her.

The next day I arrive with poems. Becky says she wants to hear Joyce Kilmer's "Trees" which she remembers from school. "I think that I shall never see/ A poem lovely as a tree,/ A tree which may in summer wear/ A nest of robins in its hair...." She's been wearing a wig since chemotherapy but no more. I stroke her hair and tell her it's grown out. "Has it?" she responds with a touch of excitement.

Her legs are skeletal. Long and angled in a v in bed. Her smile all teeth. She's stroking her neck as I read, then her right breast, cupping her hand over the place of the tumors. Her growths.

When David comes into the room, I say "Your son the writer." And she repeats in a mix of puzzlement and animation, "My son." He sits on the side of her bed, and later he tells me the image of her as a dancer won't leave his head. All in a second he sees her in a pink tutu, tights, ballet slippers, her black hair back in a bun, her dark eyes wide open, with a slight smile as she makes one twirl, then stops. That picture gone, he looks at her in bed and sees a concentration camp survivor.

Little Miss Rebecca Shapiro, child star. President of her high school debate team. Popular and proper, a rabbi's daughter. Prisoner.

In her first year of college, commuting from home to Little Rock Junior College, she couldn't make herself finish a final paper for a history class, and that was the end of school. A teacher at a dance school in Montgomery, Alabama, who had seen Becky dance as a young teenager, had taken her to live in her house for one year so she could have serious training; there are newspaper articles about Becky's dancing. But by high school her family had said no to the dancer. It wasn't proper for a lady. She became a secretary until she married her childhood sweetheart Morris. Musical and playful, she and Morris have been the local Ginger Rogers and Fred Astaire on whatever dance floor they enter.

Our daughter Judith adores her aunt and uncle. She, too, is a talented dancer, a child star in the Chattanooga dance world. She's in a dance program at Harvard this summer. When she calls complaining she won't get the classes she wants or they won't be good enough, and she's acting like a victim, I blurt, "You'd better make it happen if you're serious about being a dancer. You have a gift; acknowledge it, serve it." And I can tell by the silence that I've said something important. "Your life is holy; take it so."

Easy to tell someone else. I'm holding on to myself by pulling away to read, my old solution. This is the first July 4th vacation when, with Harold's factory closed, we have a holiday without a plan, a venture without adventure. I'm a bit afraid of it.

When we go to Dalton, I have David to talk to; he also experiences the world as a writer. We take walks; he understands my talk of hot, green stillness, how stifled I feel by this landscape of "nothing moves," though these days I'm grateful for leaving sick rooms and breathing any outside air. David is quieter than I am, and I worry that I talk too much.

We are flying to New York for a long weekend, both Harold and I flying away from Becky's illness. I didn't push to leave; I was ready to roll with the circumstances, even curious about how we'd play out the days of this non-vacation, the two of us at home together. Maybe we couldn't do it.

We decided to go away. Becky will not die in the next few days, and everyone is saying, "Harold should get away, he works so hard, he takes on so much responsibility." So I got plane tickets for the end of the week and chose a hotel for us near Central Park. A lovely choice. Pastoral, tamed nature once again, the park with the museum at its edge, Shakespeare in the Park at the Delacorte, poetic and civil.

The days are beautiful. I take my book to the park and read while Harold watches neighborhood teams play baseball. One night we see a play, *Passion*, where the knowledge of death enters when a couple's children leave home. Though freedom comes, it's going to get taken away by dying, by an urge to cling to your mate as mortality appears. As we start off the sidewalk after the play, I break into tears. Harold isn't affected by the play, doesn't think much of it. We go for dinner to an expensive Italian restaurant written up in the *Times* last week. Inside me is a tantrum wanting to surface. I order wrong. Harold takes the salad I don't like. He allows me to be irrational. I relax. The osso bucco comes, and it feels great fighting the bone for its marrow. The older man and woman sitting next to us are bickering, but when the waiter comes they smile.

Sunday is nice again in the park. In my book by Gabriel Garcia Marquez I read, "All of us will be mysteriously murdered in the sense that we don't know why we *must* die." My savage self is grateful for his company.

July 12th. We sit around waiting for Becky to die. Her daughter Carol has flown in from Connecticut to be with her mother.
Morris watches the Braves play the Phillies on TV. Harold and
Carol are in the dining room discussing mortgage rates. I'm
reading an article in the *Atlanta Journal* about Eastern Airlines
fares. David is with Becky. All day Becky moans a guttural
breath, an audible in out, holding her breath intermittently for
ten or fifteen seconds so we think this is it, and it isn't. Out
comes the tremulous gutturals over again. We wander in and
out of her room. Sometimes we're all watching TV. The Braves
just missed a catch at the bottom of the 9th and a Phillie's in for
the winning run. "It's all over," roars the announcer.

In out in out. Morris is talking to the nurse in the bedroom.
Harold's gone to sleep on the living room sofa. Carol and I get
into a conversation about film. It's her academic field; she's
writing her Ph.D. dissertation on Alfred Hitchcock and Flan-
nery O'Connor. At forty she's a bride, having married for the
first time last November. Becky's raspberry taffeta gown from
the wedding hangs in the front of the closet. And though film
interests me, it's David's talking about death, about what's in
front of our eyes, I feel kindred to right now, how he sees horror when he catches the whites of his mother's eyes as her
pupils roll back, when he watches her red-painted nails at the
end of bony fingers on the bandage at her throat.

2:30 a.m. 3:30 a.m. We wander. I go into the bedroom and
watch Morris kiss Becky and look at her for a long time, an ac-
ceptance which touches me to tears. As if sensing my empathy,
he comes to hug me. The weave of our wandering has created
a deep warmth among the five of us.

As the sun comes up we're quiet. Like a giant heartbeat
Becky's breathing holds us inside. Faint but steady breaths out
of the white face tell us she lives. The house has become a heart.
Becky has become an object.

When I hear friends nowadays talk about their time with a

dying parent, I see how it could have been different. We could have helped Becky let go. We could have sung to her, told her we knew she had to go, given her her dying. We didn't know to do that; we waited. I remember when I came from New York to the funeral parlor after Mama died, I turned to the funeral director to ask if it was all right to kiss her. What was I afraid of? Catching death? Why did I ask? Why did I have to be told?

Chilled in the early morning by air conditioning and little sleep, I must go outside for fresh air and sunlight. The birds are singing – a few weeks ago Becky complained about their noise – and there's a damp coolness to the air. I don't warm up. When I go back in, the breaths have become random. I go into the bedroom and look at Becky's body of angles and decide to draw her. For whatever reason, I'm making lines on paper. I'm numb, without affect. Obsession has taken hold of me. I re-draw the shapes. The fingers are not straight but curled like claws with red tips. One eye is closed, the right eye slit open, glassy sliver of white. There's a sudden choking. The last? – no. When Morris enters, I feel like a spy, subversive and uncaring, and put my pencil under me.

By nine a.m. Becky has 104 degrees temperature, pneumonia, the nurse announces. The day nurse is coming up the driveway. The night nurse doesn't want to leave. She knows Becky's death is imminent, and the act of dying, no matter how many deaths she's seen, is profound. Deaths at home were once part of everyone's life. I think how someone like Emily Dickinson, who was considered a recluse, would have come to the knowledge of birth and death, the most amazing events of the body, happening right in front of her eyes. By contrast, sophisticated people today may never witness such events since people are born and die in hospitals far away from home.

Becky's breaths come with a sigh now. On and on. 104 fever and blood pressure 30. At eleven o'clock we eat a big breakfast. Then I'm impatient. I must lie down next to her, draw the blinds against the eastern sun, willing darkness. But after a half hour I leave the room.

Now we're all pacing. Shadows from a dogwood tree moving on the yellow chaise make the cushions rise and fall. Her breaths drag through the whole house, pulling us to her room. Carol and I sprawl on the big bed, holding hands. The night nurse sits on its edge. Becky's been moved to a hospital bed across from us. David sits by her side. Morris stands. On the white chair to his right the day nurse sits. The only life is Becky, her in, out, in, out. I look at her face and see a bird.

By two o'clock in the afternoon Carol and I decide to go into the kitchen. We pull out leftovers to fix a salad. I open a can of tuna. The nurse rushes in, "There's a change."

We go to a new in out. The sounds growing fainter, the teeth coming closer together. Morris on her left, David and Carol on the right, Harold and I at the foot of the bed. And for the first time in many hours Becky's eyes open wide to look at Morris, a long look. Then she turns her head to look at us, and she turns again to Morris. Eyes wide open. Closed. Faint breath. No breath. We sob, the nurse who'd left us alone rushes in, puts her stethoscope to Becky, and the breathing starts up again in heavy wheezes, sob sounds, Becky's mouth now turned down, her sobs seeming to join our sobs. Startled, we stop. Her breath is faint, her mouth now shaped to an open cupid's bow. Stop. A shrug of her right shoulder, up, forward, a crook of sound. Gurgle. And nothing. The stethoscope. The nurse saying, "I'm sorry."

We turn to each other, taking turns in each other's arms. Then Harold is going out of the room, bringing back a prayer book, and he's chanting the Kaddish at the foot of his sister's bed. He's his father standing there saying the prayer for the dead that praises life. The ritual brings order into the room. When it's over, our sobs return; we move around the room, our sounds sometimes so deep I think of laughter.

We leave Becky to the nurses in the room. David goes to the phone to make calls. Morris and Carol return to stare at a crossword puzzle on the table until attendants from the funeral home come with their gurney and wheel Becky from her room, covered by a green chenille throw. Morris cries. David, who runs in from the other room, sees the van pull away. "I guess I've seen enough," he despairs.

What is it about money and possessions that enters the family dynamic after someone's death? We are not a petty family, nor are we financially needy, yet my sister and I, after Mama died, bickered over money. Mama had given Raina money to help her buy a bookstore, and Raina was paying her back. Mama lived comfortably but was by no means rich, and after the expenses of her illness, she had very little in the bank when she died. I felt that half the remaining money Raina owed Mama was mine. I had to say so, that she could send half of it monthly as she'd sent to Mama. Then she insisted on sending me my half all at once, implying if I must have it, here it is. And I did want it, half of what was Mama's to me.

After Becky died, when I returned from running errands for Carol who was to go through her mother's belongings before flying home, I saw she put aside the lace cloth we had bought in Spain. I picked it up to look at it, maybe to claim it, and Carol said, "It's so beautiful, I want it." I put it down. But I'm angry. In the other room I cry, then try to calm myself. Earlier Carol had given us a tea set, saying she'd keep another set she liked better, and I felt a twinge of annoyance then. Why say you're giving something because you like it less? Harold tells Carol about my feelings (they're his too, but mine are out there), and she comes to apologize. We hug.

I should be doing for others, for the brother who is my husband, for Becky's daughter who is my niece; yet I feel so needy. To handle my anger, to get away from it, I call the director of the Dalton Creative Arts Guild. I've wanted to bring her a catalog of a New York painter in her eighties, Edith Bry, whose show I went to see at NYU's Gray Gallery. It's miraculous the way speaking about the artist returns me to a strong self. My life these three years has built inside me a way of finding order so that, even when I'm flailing, I can count on not remaining lost.

The night Becky died I had a dream in which I'm in Bruges. Awake I can't remember a thing about it except the name of the city, and I think how strange, Bruges, a word I've never said, a place I've never thought to go. Belgium. It means nothing to me. Bruges, that place will continue to haunt me. Eleven years after this summer of Becky's dying when, as my birthday is about to happen and I'm living in New York, I'll travel to discover how a dream, Bruges, one word from the night, can be held inside for a long time, then given birth.

This morning, as I write these pages, I remember how I struggled to bring the parts of myself together after Becky died. So unlike this morning when I wake from two lovely dreams of harmony: in the first dream Harold and I are flying on Republic Airlines to Denmark. We're in coach. First class and coach are across from each other. First class is for business people; they are laughing around the table across from us. The flight attendants are jolly and helpful to us all. I look out the window and see a blonde stewardess, who is pregnant, swimming in the air. The air is water. First class passengers have the privilege of swimming out to kiss her belly. I'm perfectly content to watch it happen. I wake smiling and drift off again to a large, very dark woman trying to get on the elevator in my building. I'm in it and the door is almost closed, open just a crack. As she attempts to enter, I push the door-open button, carefully, consciously, because, in haste, it is easy to push door-close. The door opens; she enters, and I am happy to have been composed.

These dreams come this morning of my grandson's fourth birthday. It is also the Memorial Day holiday. Birth and death, light and dark move inside me now in tandem. Writing toward the fourth sublet, I am coming to an ending. In these sublets I gave birth to myself in the middle of my life; I extended my foot for the slipper that fit. That act enabled me to enter an elevator and, with my finger, reach for the door-open button, saying yes even to the entry of a large darkness.

But that summer of 1983 when Becky died, I struggled to find peace. I couldn't make up my mind about anything. Even driving a car I'd pull into a parking lot and weave between two spaces, unable to decide where to park. Copying my poems one day in Harold's office, I looked at them in my hand; they seemed foolish pieces of paper. I'd just been given a tour of a new machine Harold had bought for his factory, a huge converter that turned petroleum pellets into rolling sheets of plastic film, and my small poems – what did they matter?

When we first moved to Chattanooga in 1964, I remember our being invited by a local artist to join her and her husband, an older couple, on their boat on Lake Chickamauga, and as we cruised she told me about being decisive. "In a restaurant," she said, "I know immediately what to order." To me that was an amazing statement. At the time – I was in my early thirties – I always ordered by waiting to see what others chose, not to choose what someone else wanted, but, on the contrary, to order what hadn't been chosen. I wanted to see every possibility. Either way had nothing to do with my body. I remember afterward understanding that I was being given a lesson by an artist. I envied her, her body's knowing it wanted veal, not fish. *Her body's knowing.*

Eventually I learned to think with my body, but, remembering once it was otherwise, I never take knowledge or process for granted. In every generation there's a freedom to be won; that's what we read at the Passover seder, and I take it personally, the idea of undiscovered freedoms. Dreams are my messengers; they get me to pay attention. And travel is exploration, the going forth a pilgrimage. Both acts take me toward discovery.

I held on to the dream word, Bruges, after Becky died, and though years went by before I was ready to take the message, I acted on it. What I managed to do after Becky's death, even in my state of disorganization, came from experience during the previous summers. I knew to get myself to a poetry workshop. In August I went to the Napa Valley Writer's Conference in California. Galway Kinnell was going to be there as well as several of my peers from the NYU program.

I arrive at the workshop in my disparate state. When offered a chance to join a group reading, I say no, thinking I want to work on new poems, then regret my decision fifteen minutes later, when I remember how much it meant to me to recite my poems to an audience in the spring.

Sitting with my friend Frannie before our first workshop session with the poet Sandra McPherson, musing on how we're no longer beginners, how we've come out to the public, giving readings, sending work to journals, I startle both of us by saying, "Now we're visible, open to a shot in the back. Now we're targets." That statement is so unlike me. Probably Becky's death has left me vulnerable, feeling unprotected.

We go into class, and a man decides to make me a target. My poem "The Hollowed Bread" is the first one up for comments after our break. It's a new poem about watching Julia Child on TV, and it's raw, the way I've been trained by Galway to present in workshop. Discussion begins with praise for the lines "with throaty assurance/ she cuts the heart/ out of the round loaf," which makes me happy because I just added those words.

"The worst lines in the poem," I hear from a man across the room. "It's not helpful to Myra to praise her falsely."

Others rush to my defense, but I can hardly hear because their sympathy is so strong it's arousing self-pity in me. The man has to defend himself; we hear a lecture on weakness in a poem and his contempt for soft responses in criticism.

"The word 'tiny' to describe the sandwiches, now that's sentimental," he continues, and I hear some class agreement which prompts him to persist with generalities about flabby poems. At this point I find my voice and ask him to stay with particulars since he's taking up my time with his general attack.

Sandra McPherson, the poet leading the workshop, has not intervened or said a word. I feel cheated and assaulted. My fifteen minutes are up; we're on to another poem, and as I quiet down, I begin to cry. The quieter I get the more I seem to cry. I keep my head down. At the end of class the man comes over to my seat and apologizes.

"Oh no you don't," I say immediately, "No, don't do that." With anger I tell him he's got to claim what he's said, he can't take it back now. "One opinion was in order, but three, four, a continual barrage? You took over…." The end of that thought I don't get out, I start to cry. "I hate this," I say, "I don't want to respond this way."

He's unnerved, says he and three other guys decided during break to be tougher, only they deserted him so he had to carry the thrust himself. I'm crying, he's questioning if he made me cry, and he backs away since I can't speak. Women rush around to comfort me – I sob as the sympathy mounts. A woman who hears the account of the three sworn to toughness announces "gang rape" – and I almost faint.

"You began to heave, like a child," Frannie tells me when we have lunch.

"I'm humiliated," I say, "I can't believe I broke down. I was like the hors d'oeuvre in my poem, a bread offering its own insides."

Well, raw poems are just that. Frannie and I talk about learning self-defense. "We've been spoiled by good teachers," I say, though I don't believe in being spoiled by good teaching. "Maybe I should take karate to learn to concentrate my mind and strengthen my body." I know I must learn to be out there, to be articulate when I'm angry; the tough kid from the Bronx must become a strong woman. Feeling powerless – my poems as insignificant sheets of paper – is not appropriate. Frannie remembers Sharon Olds telling her, "Be a god." That's appropriate.

My good fortune is having Galway invite those of us from the NYU program to join Robert Hass and him for dinner that night. I end up at the head of the table, Galway to my left. He treats us to a good bottle of Cabernet. I tell a long story about the trip to Greece with Robert Bly. I'm back in full voice. Others tell their travel stories. We're a group of poets speaking, listening, and laughing together. These writers with their generosity and good company bring out the precarious best in me.

Fourth Sublet

The Village, 1983–84

I'VE ALWAYS SAID that schools and bathrooms save me. I have escaped from the work of children and household with the words, "Excuse me, I am going to use the bathroom." And when I spend time and money to go to school, no one in my family denies its importance.

It is understood that I'll return to the city in the early fall of '83 to continue my studies in the new writing department at New York University. In summer, on the trip to New York with Harold, I'd found my fourth sublet. With only a few days to look for an apartment and nothing good turning up in the *Village Voice* or the *New York Times*, I'd used a real estate broker. I had to tell her the neighborhood I wanted. From my first three sublets, in the West Village, the Upper West Side, and Gramercy Park, I knew I liked the Village best, its small streets and lower buildings, its funky grid, its history, the mix of artists, students, and people of all ages who fill the streets. I liked the buzz at night when I was out. It felt adult, not domestic, and the remove of the Village from midtown let me feel I wasn't on vacation in New York City, I lived there.

The sublet I chose turned out to be neither artistic nor filled with Village character. The broker took me to an apartment owned by people who lived in Florida; I didn't think they used the place at all. It had pseudo French provincial furniture, the kind you see in hotel rooms. It was clean and spacious – Harold immediately liked it – and it had wonderful light. On the eighth floor of a white, post-war building, it faced south over rooftops with a view down Mercer Street toward Soho. I knew I would have sun during the day and, at night, street life, a bracelet of lit-up traffic flowing towards the harbor. Ninth Street was attractive and close to New York University. I took it.

It's September 21, 1983. This summer of Becky's death was sad and difficult. Now I enter the apartment and it looks sub-urban to me, all that fake glitz, so I drop my luggage and hit the streets just to feel the city before I go to class. I see there are many small shops, artistic and chic, around the corner on University, and, right on my corner, a lively restaurant with Al Hirschfield drawings of theatre actors and writers on the walls. I stop for a light supper.

My class at NYU is in a building just two blocks away. This term I'm auditing a poetry class on craft taught by Joseph Brodsky, the Russian exile and future Nobel prize winner in literature. He has the reputation of being hard on students – no nonsense. This first night I get to class early for what I know will be a crowded room; it's a hot evening, and I'm sweating from the humidity and my anxiety as I find a seat. I glance around to see familiar faces.

Brodsky begins. Praising Thomas Hardy he says something about Hardy's line on Shelley's "To a Skylark," something about "a pinch of dust." My head is pounding. Brodsky stutters so one has to be patient, to relax. I wish I could. Then the room gets quiet as we watch him write on the board: "Some think they are strong, some think they are smart,/ Like _ _ _ they are pulled apart./ America can break your heart."

"Fill in the empty three syllable space," he instructs.

I write "dogs in heat."

"Butterflies," he says.

We get a lecture on heft and ease, on contrast, on the lightness that "butterflies" fulfills. I'm ashamed of my stupid phrase, my heavy hand. In his voice I hear familiar blame, the kind of disdain I heard in the house of my Russian family. I sit in an old defiance. I should feel humble in this great man's presence, but the anger of my childhood-self rises.

When I get back to the apartment – a space without love, a table in the dining area with European pretensions – I can't unpack. I know my books and colorful shawls draped over chairs will warm the place, but I'm not in the mood to turn on the charm. Within a few days I'll call my friend Ingrid who also lives on 9th Street, three blocks east, and she'll be welcoming, decisive, and helpful. "Buy tea, buy plants," she'll say.

On the weekend, sun coming through the windows, my thoughts go to Harold, why I first wanted to be with him, what he is to me. I think comfort, how easy like a brother he was from the start. Never having had a brother, I was puzzled by boys. I'd read articles in magazines about how they would want me more if I didn't come on too strong and talked about what interested them. Harold was a relief; I didn't have to play those games, my heart could slow down. Once I took him shopping for the college dance he'd invited me to, and, better than my mother, he helped me choose the right dress, a pink chiffon strapless that floated and belied my confusion.

I want less chaos. What I think Galway Kinnell means by being selfless. Less ego, more calm. Maybe this year I'll learn how to let go, how to flow. In Brodsky's class I sit like the coarse Bronx kid, all will, full of ambition and aggression.

In the way of my past three sublets, I do get around to making the apartment mine by going through each room, each cabinet. The towels and sheets are nice. The kitchen has modern appliances. The cheesy art on the walls, geometric faces à la Picasso, I take down.

I work on a new poem for the first writing class. Sharon Olds, alternating with Carolyn Forché, will lead it. I'm glad to be working with Sharon again; she tries to create Galway's sense of camaraderie, and as a woman she is both strong and nurturing. But I continue to be anxious, even numb; it's hard to write or read. I can think of myself as an empty vessel, a lady in waiting. Whom will I serve? Aha, there's my start on selflessness.

I'll tend a garden. I've gone to the greenmarket at Union Square to buy plants; three of them I arrange on a glass shelf to catch the bright sunlight. And when I look at each pot, the one with long, lettuce-like leaves, not as dark as romaine, rippled at the edges, the one with spotted leaves, and the one with ivy trailing towards the wall, which I water so it will relax and spread, I become less scared, even content.

In Sharon's class I talk about death. New talk for me. My poem "Out Shopping" tries to create the sensation of sudden loss, my wallet snatched from my purse with no sign of danger. And simultaneously it reflects my sense of time, of aging. My ear lobes in the mirror become suddenly my mother-in-law's hanging flesh. "My wallet gone without a shiver/or a sign. We need to know./ We teach a child to hear the tick/tock of the clock, to witness/ where the big and small hands go."

To the class I mention my recent thoughts on humility, that maybe it's about getting old and knowing I'm going to die. And since that's recent conscious knowledge, that I'm in this second half of my life which holds my death, shouldn't my work match that revelation? "Should it hold less concrete matter?" I ask. Someone suggests that for now my desire for selflessness is enough, the right poems will come.

A friend has invited me to a breakfast for the writer May Sarton at an apartment on the Upper West Side. Sarton's books, especially her *Journal of a Solitude*, have been important to me, giving me permission to love being alone, to think about who I am when I am alone and to call it freedom and adventure.

"We must serve life," she's telling us, a circle of writers seated near her, "the pheasant who comes into my garden, its cry, the paintings of Manet at the Metropolitan." I like her mentioning both animal and human natures, bridging her Maine with our New York. She urges us to render those events outside ourselves that move us. "Open your eyes and your ears...."

Sarton, a large, sturdy-looking, gray-haired woman, has just turned seventy. She talks about age, and it's the first time I've heard anyone speak of it as just one more stage of life to live into, with curiosity for what it can provide. "Never mind facts, names, and places," she says about memory loss. "Associations, images are the stuff of the imagination; they yield to take us deeper." Toward the end of the breakfast, she speaks of silence, how it's our pathway to deep memory, to the riches of the past from which to create the new; in silence, time's on our side.

Inspired and excited by that nice irony, I get on the subway to go back to the Village. When I change to the R train at 42nd Street and walk toward an empty seat, I hesitate, seeing the woman sitting next to it. Is it her long, gray hair in disarray? She has a distraught look. For just a second I pause, then sit.

"How many stops to Princeton Street?" she asks me. I'm puzzled and say I don't know that street. She looks at a note in her purse and corrects herself, "Prince Street." I say it's the stop after I get off.

"What is your name?" she asks, startling me, but I let her engage me. I tell her my name and sense she would like to tell me hers. She would like to feel less a stranger. She tells me she's Persis Ballou from Concord, Mass. Immediately I'm struck by the magic of such a name. She looks for a card in her purse.

I must come to Concord and she will show me around. In the short time it takes to get to my stop at 8th Street, I hear her story. She's in New York to play viola with the Boston Philharmonic. One month ago her husband died.

"I've written a poem," she says. We've had time for me to tell her I write poems, to which she lights up for the first time in our conversation. It prompts her to remember with sudden joy, "In college I was an English major." Then tears, as she begins to tell me a poem came to her in the hospital where her husband had been for two months. "He was too young to die." I touch her hand and wish her strength as I leave the train at 8th Street.

Old age and death are certainly walking toward me during this sublet in the city. Never before have I felt an urgency to allow them a place. Now they're arriving like invitations to somewhere new.

Today I am in love with a word. *Volute*. A spiral-shaped form, the dictionary says. I've come across it in a book about Michelangelo, the curve of his bridge that so serenely spans the Arno.

Although serenity and quiet grace are strange concepts in this chaotic city, it is in cities that the word takes shape for me. *Volute*. Stone scrolls on an old building I pass as I walk along Broadway. And yesterday I thought of the word when I looked at the paintings of Manet at the Metropolitan Museum. I got on a subway, and in three stops I was there, standing in room after room of Manet's paintings, a retrospective of his work. Caught by a detail, a volute, I marveled at oranges half-peeled, the skin curling down, the sensuous curve hanging from the orange.

I've spent the evening with two women to whom I can convey my love of a word. Last week we attended a symposium on W. H. Auden, organized by Joseph Brodsky. Sitting in the Figaro Cafe on Bleecker, I tell them about Brodsky's exercise, his request for a word in a Hardy poem. I bring up my obsession with *volute* and talk of serenity, how hard it is to achieve except through aloneness which enables you to enter the whole world slowly. Then, laughing, I admit how good it is to be among others to say so.

Brodsky is devoting most of the craft class to W. H. Auden, and I'm enjoying a poet I hardly know. Auden's contemporary, T. S. Eliot, is the poet I was taught to revere; he was clearly the star of my undergraduate, modern literature classes in Chattanooga, yet I felt he would never have liked me. I was akin to his Rachel nee Rabinovitch in "Sweeney Among the Nightingales," grabbing for what I needed. I am not Eliot's aristocratic ideal. With Auden, there is humor and an earthiness that makes me comfortable; I'm memorizing his "Musee des Beaux Arts": "About suffering they were never wrong./ The Old Masters: how well they understood/ Its human position: how it takes place/ While someone else is eating or opening a window or just walking dully along...." And though I can't say I'm relaxed in Brodsky's class, it's good getting to know Auden, his poems and his world. I've walked over to St. Marks Place, just a few blocks from my sublet, to see where he lived. It's the street of my debut reading last spring.

At the Auden symposium, Christopher Isherwood, Auden's life-long friend, laughed about their being ten-year-old schoolboys together. "The rest of our lives," he said, "we were playing grown-ups, an adventure played out by boys, a charade." That's how I often feel since I've come to New York. Whenever I make tea and sit alone at my window with my cup and teapot eight floors above the ground, I feel I'm playing house with my doll named Gloria, acting out my best dream. Any minute my mother will call me down for dinner.

That thought startles me. In my current house she would be calling from the grave. But last week, seeing Christopher Isherwood, hearing him tell such intimate stories about Auden in my own neighborhood, it was about being alive, about bringing the dead to life. At such times I am so happy I have to

pinch myself to make sure my life is real. I never take being
here for granted.

About a month after I settle into the new sublet, Harold is
visiting for the weekend, and we read in the *Times* of the death
of Mordecai Kaplan, the founder of Reconstructionist Judaism
and the father of Judith Kaplan Eisenstein whom we met when
we lived in Chicago. Her husband, Ira Eisenstein, was the rabbi
at Anshe Emet, the synagogue we attended in Chicago.

As we read about Kaplan's death, we're riding the bus uptown to Central Park; it's a mild November day, and we've
planned to walk in the park, then go to the Metropolitan Museum. "The synagogue's on 86th Street," I say. "Let's go."

Both Harold and I feel a kinship to this man who changed
the way we could be together in our observance of Judaism.
So we cross town and enter the crowded synagogue Kaplan
founded. From up in the balcony, I look down to see Judith, the
oldest of his four daughters, and her husband. It's over twenty-
five years since Chicago. We knew each other such a short time,
yet this family is important to my life; it's extraordinary to be
in their presence.

We met Rabbi Eisenstein just after I'd given birth to Karen.
In a strange way he was a mentor to me, or a muse, when I
needed such an infusion of warm, male intelligence. A New
Yorker, he was as new to Chicago as we were. That first fall of
being a mother, I went with Harold to synagogue for the high
holidays. Harold, the son of a rabbi, was at home with religious liturgy while I, the child of Marxists and non-observant
Jews, had never felt a connection to synagogue services (the
culture of Judaism, yes – *Yiddishkayt* we called it– but never to
organized religion). I followed Harold to services as a good
wife and perhaps to be part of a community. We went to the
Reconstructionist synagogue, that first holiday in Chicago, on

the recommendation of friends. I'd never heard of the Reconstructionist movement, its belief in Judaism as an ongoing, evolving civilization. For the first time I felt inspired by a religious service, and we became part of the young couples' club. People talked about literature; it felt kindred. I went to classes given by Ira Eisenstein. I remember once he gave me a ride home, asking me questions about my life, and he listened with what seemed genuine interest. I knew no men except Harold who did that.

Eisenstein's wife, Judith, was a musicologist. They had two daughters, and she had a profession equal to her husband's – that was rare in the fifties and not part of my experience. Unable to figure out how to be happy as a wife and mother, unsatisfied by the life I was living, I remember complaining and Judith Eisenstein responding, "To everything there is a season." It was a moment's exchange, we were standing in line for something. I don't know why those words consoled me, but they did. Maybe it was their poetry. Years later, when we lived down South and our second daughter was born, we named her Judith. I wanted to give her a strong name that suggested intelligence and the arts and the women like Judith Eisenstein I so admired.

Here are Judith and Ira Eisenstein standing before us again. Someone has just spoken of Kaplan's daughters, how Judith was the first girl to have been given the ceremony of Bat Mitzvah, the rite of passage from childhood to adulthood, up to her time reserved only for boys.

Vivid and vital. I hear those words in the eulogy to describe Mordecai Kaplan's ideas. I have been drifting with my own thoughts, but I listen to what is being said about Kaplan's making events vivid through the imagination and giving them life by honoring them as vital. A favorite passage from *Genesis* is read about Jacob who "took a stone and set it up as a pillar," and I hear its message of transformation, reconstruction, and how, for me, it is also a way to think of writing. Words hold the past, and we give them new strength, a new shape, by what we choose to remember and the way we use them. We can redeem the past and how we live with it. A *re-mattering*.

May Sarton, Mordecai Kaplan. In the first months of my new sublet in New York I am blessed with such models. If I stay healthy and live long like Sarton at seventy and Kaplan who was over one hundred, time will be fertile, generative, a magical replenishing. It suits me to think that an aging Myra can be fruitful and multiply. But how? How far will I go to give myself places of silence, places where poetry lives and nurtures me? Should I be separating myself even more from the family I created? What new life am I capable of producing?

Having shared the memorial with Harold is an experience I connect to how he and I are building life together in New York, how we are becoming part of the fluidity of the city, its movement: a bus ride to the Met we change into an honoring and deeply felt communion, all by way of consciousness and the ability to transfer buses.

The week after Harold leaves, I'm sitting in Leo's Luncheon-ette on 86th Street with my cousin Sophie; we've been to a reading at the 92nd Street Y in its new 1983-84 season. It's the first time she's joined me for an event since I took the new sub-let. Even though it's over a month away, we want to talk about holiday plans because Harold and Judith will be coming to New York before the three of us fly to Amsterdam for the De-cember holiday and New Years. Suddenly a woman starts screaming from the back of the restaurant. Her voice is pitched high, she's ranting, "I want to eat. All I want is something to eat. I don't want to wait."

As the waiter, a man in his sixties in a regulation black and white waiter's uniform, comes to take our order, she appears, somehow driven from the back to midway in the room. I'm giving my order so I can't see more than her maroon coat and knit cap and a wild flailing. Of course, it's disturbing and we're shaken. My voice halts, the waiter forgets my choice of entree. She keeps screaming, "I want to eat, I have a class and they won't feed me."

Sophie says she's lost her senses. They'll just try to get her out of the restaurant. In New York City fashion we go back to our own business, her son-in-law's Christmas party in Brooklyn Heights, Sophie's whole family driving down from Boston.

Again, the woman cries out. She's come back for her umbrella. It's right near us. I can see her. Young. In her twenties. A bit heavy, straight hair poking out of the cap, around her round face. A child in rage. Screaming for what she needs, for justice, for attention. "Feed me. You have to feed me." No one will listen. And the voice goes higher as if it will throw itself out and on and over everything, as if its wild energy provides the warmth of arms and a blanket.

I can resurrect that woman from deep in my body. She is my child-self. And when I hear her, all the years after feel like the thinnest veneer. Umbrella in her hand, flapping in the air, she's out the door, but she stays so real to me. Last Passover I held her in my poem's words "how will I out to speak a rage/ rising? On my milk-white plate/ a coral cobra's running wild."

During my conference with Sharon Olds this week, she told me, "You have your voice. Only one thing to tell you now: let the passion heat up and open." Open to that wildness?! After the Olds conference, back at my apartment, I wrote:

But passion. Ahhhh,
      no wonder I am greedy and
      make demands.
Without wonder I am pushed into a corner of my life.

Do I mean "without wildness" instead of wonder? What is the real wildness I want to satisfy? How to do the dance of grace *and* passion? I think back to the night before I married, the moment in the corner where I held myself, crying, some return to the child the world wanted to tame. How to be full of strong particularity, and civilize it to make a life with others?

A few days later, when I have my conference with Carolyn Forché, I'm still thinking about passion and wildness. Forché isn't a person to engage. Going through my poems, she seems to find me uninteresting. I feel dismissed. In her last class she urged us to have adventures, to travel to troubled places. Her poems have done that. Yet in our own experience with her, she seems a baby. She's afraid of NYU stairways at night and asked us to hold our workshops in people's apartments. Someone has to walk her back to her place after class. But after our conference she's off to Lebanon; her journalist boyfriend is there.

Okay, she's making her way, moving forward however she needs to do it. That's what I'm doing too. And what she's contributed to my knowledge is what kind of woman makes me nuts. The seductress, the one who captivates and leads you to think she cares about you, then pulls away. Seeing how Galway Kinnell, the director of the program, has encouraged community, Forché wants to go along: "Let's all go roller skating," she exclaims one evening, and later, "Let's get together for a weekend retreat." We go, she doesn't show up. I begin to strain to please her, thinking there is something I need to do to make us work better together. It's the come-on of my mother, her desire to be giving with the desire to be elsewhere, the inability to deliver.

She's certainly stirred up my insecurities. At first I was excited by her co-teaching with Sharon. I wanted to be in the presence of a political poet. Now I see her as building a life around events, throwing herself toward danger in a kind of notorious way. My lurching at events, my going forth secure with a husband behind the scenes, may make me an older version of her. Maybe our child-selves are alike. Well, what I do know now is who leads me to new poems, and judging by that measure, Forché is no good for me.

Harold and Judith and I enter 1984 in the Netherlands. In the dark winter of Amsterdam, I find warmth in the way houses and shops share the same facades, fit tight against each other, confronting the water which is everywhere.

The sensation of union disappears inside the Anne Frank house. We move apart, as if knowledge here *requires* separation. Maybe it's because this is a house of death, of a family's struggle to live only to die. It's not actually the Frank house; it's an attic over a store where the Franks had to hide from the Nazis. There are many other people touring these rooms, reading the documents, yet it is absolutely quiet. What we feel we can't share; we need silence. People's extreme cruelty and deprivation and kindness and romance and bad luck reside all in this one building: to be forced to hide for over two years only to be captured less than a year before the war's end, to survive the concentration camp only to die one month before liberation. We visit this house of death because a girl's words live. Her words are pushing all of us in the room to knowledge, and a strange and powerful isolation.

On this vacation, I am too often moving through the hours of family life without being fully present to Harold and Judith. I love what I see, the energy I feel from reading and planning and getting to where the maps tell me I'll be, but then, too often, I become mechanical.

If I were alone, I think I would be different. Maybe I would do less. I would be pure Myra though. Is there such a thing? Maybe as we die. In childbirth I remember how, in primal pain, Harold by my side until the delivery, I became quiet, held myself to myself, refusing to scream, and the baby took her time pushing herself out of me; when there was nothing for me to do but push, my body did it while my mind went elsewhere.

birth/death

Nothing is like birth except maybe death. In everyday life, when I become distant from myself, I chatter. To survive chaos or too many feelings at one time or too many people, I zzzzz like a wire that has short-circuited or flail like a horse gone mad. Only now that I write have I found the way to center, a harness to quiet and contain me. How good it is to have the fitting thing to ask for. On the last morning of 1983, I tell Harold and Judith I want to stay in the room while they go down to breakfast together.

I love knowing the steps to take to keep me living the life that wants to live in me. Sitting on the window seat, looking out at the steel gray water, I write. I'm trying to reconstruct the dream I had. In it, Harold and I were flying to separate places; we take separate shuttle buses to get to our particular counters. On my bus I realize I've left my black snakeskin pocketbook at home; on the plane whose first stop is Athens, Ohio, I realize I've also left my dresses and shoes. I have only the white sandals I'm wearing. The young women I'm traveling with are wearing the new style open-front dresses so their small breasts are exposed. I'll call the black woman at home and have her forward my things, but when I call, I forget to have her send clothes and ask only for the black pocketbook. I'm not unhappy, just scattered. Is that a picture of what I imagine without Harold? Darkness? And what of snakeskin, shed skin? But it is a scenario of both white and black, both elements visualized toward the start of the new year. Maybe I'm acknowledging I'll carry the knowledge of death, by choice now.

While I'm writing and thinking about the dream, the sun comes out, a rarity in Amsterdam on winter mornings. I have to smile, taking it as a blessing.

Harold and Judith are at the door. We'll walk along the

canals this sunny day, the last day of this year that has brought to our family new death and life.

Gborn gven: two words I wake from next day, the first day of 1984. When I look out the window, I see the concrete pilings under a bridge and over it birds flying. The dream words sound like combined English-Yiddish or some guttural language saying "You were born, birth happened to you." They don't add "and you will die." No, not on this first day of 1984; they speak of the gift of life, and I sense I am to make the passive tense active.

In my sublet after our December vacation in Amsterdam, Judith about to go back to college for her last semester, class of 1984, I'm reading and I remark with envy, "Tom Stoppard's life is so unified." He's a playwright I'm not particularly fond of because too often I find him just clever and wordy, too mindful for me, but I'm getting high on his life as I read an article about him in the Sunday *Times*.

Judith, noticing my laughter and pleasure, asks what I'm reading. When I tell her what a good life Stoppard has, how together he is, she challenges my perception, "It's kind of simple-minded to think one magazine article would convey the complexity of a life. You're gullible."

I'd never thought about how completely I give myself to what I read, as if it were gospel; I never examined that. I like being challenged by Judith, having daughters who open my eyes and make me think.

Judith and I were once of one mind, or so it seemed to me, extremely simpatico. Suddenly that's not true anymore. It's something I have to get used to. More and more I feel her resistance. When I say, "What are you doing today?" she won't answer, or she'll ask what I said as if she doesn't hear me. Finally I say, "Why don't you tell me not to ask you such questions, that you'd rather not discuss your plans or whatever," and she proceeds to do just that, "I'd rather not discuss...."

Later when I give her advice about her girlfriend who's coming to spend the night, possibly leaving her to go out on a date, and I suggest it's not an act of friendship to be left for a man, Judith says, "Maybe I have a plan and you don't know about it. Maybe I'm like Dad, I live in the present, and I don't have to deal with it until it happens."

"Okay," I say, "give me behavior rules. I take it you don't want questions or advice."

"Right," she says, kind of sheepishly.

Judith and I each want our separate lives, yet there's been such pleasure in our closeness, in our shared interests. For me being with her has been a union with my best self, the joy of me with an ideal ME. I have created that vision which I know I have to withdraw; it's the way of a parent who wants to recreate in her own child the life she would have wished for. If she blooms, I bloom.

Here we are at 1984, that fictional, futuristic year. If any year has epitomized a new order, this one is it. Judith will have a world I can't know. From early on, she'll be allowed the freedom and education to go her separate ways, to live wherever she wants, to become whatever she wants, with support from parents. It's a dream I can't conceive of as anything but good. What I don't foresee is that it's my dream, a dream enhanced by its contrast to immigrant life and the inequality of women I come from. It's painful separating my vision from my daughter's, even as I want her independence, even as I've created a good place of my own in the world. I don't want to imagine my despair if I hadn't made it to my work and to this city.

Well, it's new to me to think my dream may not be my daughters'. Letting go of old behaviors is always tricky; you don't even know they exist until you know. Getting these glimpses of our separation and struggle, it's just come to me that I provide no model from my young life for the one my daughters are living. I was married at Judith's age!

Karen is across the country, so I don't see how she lives her life; I can let go more easily. She's always been the independent child, the older sister, and I let myself assume she'll handle whatever happens.

Again the thought surfaces, what if I have to die for my children to come to their true selves? I don't know why I didn't begin writing steadily until my mother died. Now that scares me. Suddenly that fact puts a burden on how I perceive my daughters' struggles. I don't want to die for a long time, but I don't want to hold back my children's lives. "Let me live," I want to call out, and "please don't let me stop you."

What if this is not neurosis? In literature there are many stories of displacement. The classic is the father-son account of how Oedipus kills a stranger on the road who turns out to be his father, then becomes king himself. That he marries his mother is perhaps a boy's story. For mother-daughter there's Demeter and Persephone. The daughter must go off, have her underground life though it means death to the life she's left behind. When she returns, bringing spring, a new way of living begins. Separate, then together. Girls don't seem to have to murder their mothers. Pandemonium and tasks and separation, yes, but eventually there's reunion. Literature makes me happy.

Eager to begin the 1984 winter-spring semester at NYU, I'm certain my excitement comes from knowing I'll again be in a workshop led by Galway Kinnell. Galway's definitely the poet who helps me break through to my strongest poems.

And I'm back to the pleasure of memorizing great poems from the tradition. I've chosen Gerard Manley Hopkins' "God's Grandeur." On the subway I have to be careful not to miss my stop, staying with Hopkins' delicious language, getting it right:

"It will flame out, like shining from shook foil;/ It gathers to a greatness like the ooze of oil/ Crushed."

Galway, first night in class, instructs us, "Choose to memorize poems with muscularity, with awkward, intricate language." The word *muscularity* interests me. I'm not sure what he means. I'm thinking it's a masculine virtue. How do I make it mine? Yet I sense Galway is saying something that I need to know.

During this same time I've begun a movement class. Last semester, at a party for writers in the NYU program, I watched some of the women dance and envied the inventive ways they gave their bodies to the music, how good it looked seeing each woman gyrate here, there, so wholeheartedly and uniquely fluid. I told Sharon Olds how much I would like to move like that, jerk and slide, the gusto of it, and she said she'd been going to a wonderful movement teacher, Jack Wiener, who runs the School for Creative Movement. She thought I'd like him. So I've called and signed up to begin with some private sessions.

During the first meeting Jack puts on music and asks me to move to it any way I want. I try to forget he's watching and, with my eyes closed, let myself into the music. I can't do it for long; self-consciousness sets in. I suggest we both dance, that way I won't feel like a looked-at object. As we dance, I begin to cry. For happiness? For release? To stop myself from continuing? At the end of class, Jack says, "You hold in, you keep reining your emotions, holding your breath. Release the emotion. Break out of your body. What is yours will be yours, asserted. Affirmed."

When I leave I feel good, I do feel release. I take myself to a new restaurant on St. Marks Place, an intimate, candlelit room, and order delicious veal piccata. The waiter, to celebrate the opening of the place, offers me a glass of white wine. I join the celebration.

With these movement classes, *muscularity* takes on lucid focus. When Jack says I rise on my bones instead of my muscles, I don't even know what he means at first; it takes a while for me to distinguish those parts of my body. But then muscularity grows from metaphor to become physical fact as I feel the sides of my legs, the muscles there, support me as I walk, the muscles in my arms tangible now as I lift a book. It will change the way I breathe, and that will enter my poems, new breaths eliciting new line breaks and phrasing.

Physical awareness will enter my dreams. The night I dream I'm in the city of Paris, I wake having held a city inside me. Awake, I realize Paris is also a person, a man, Homer's Paris. Knowing that, I want to begin a poem, and I play with both city and man. The city seems the enterprise of men in love with women, building her out of a longing for expression, for beauty. As I work on the poem I title "A Brother," I explore the muse as male, as counterpart to the female muse in the traditional world of male artists.

I'm excited by this new poem, and when I bring it to class so are Galway and the others. With class suggestions I keep working. I'm held by the line: "Everything I loved within my room stayed/ visible." Like a word from a dream, I carry *visible* with me through the week until it seems to say *physical*. I smile knowing the task is to make what's in my body visible, make poems. Memories lodged in my muscles crave expression. Words begin to walk toward me; *crave* makes me see *carve*, and I build.

As I work with the image of a brother as male muse, I remember a story by Doris Lessing that I read years ago. In it a brother and sister meet regularly to make love, but they never allow orgasm. They move away from each other just before the moment of climax. Intense passion is what they achieve, without a consummation. Life without death, I thought, when I first read this shocking story. Now in my mind it's a story in which Lessing may have wanted to unite, not merge, male and female, a male inside a female, the male muse.

I can't remember the name of the story, and I want to reread it, but my books by Doris Lessing are in Chattanooga. I go to the Strand, its seven miles of used books three blocks from me, but I don't find her book of short stories so I walk east to St. Marks Bookstore, and it's there. When I get home, I skim to find the story, then seduced by Lessing's good writing, I read story after story until I come to "Each Other."

"I suppose your brother is coming again?" it begins. In this opener the question is posed by the woman's husband. "He might," she replies. And when the husband wants to press her further, "What do you mean, he might?" she doesn't answer but holds up her hand "to inspect five pink arrows." With that gesture we're in the realm of Venus and Cupid. And when I come to the end of the first long paragraph which sums up the anxiety of husband and wife, I put myself in her place as I read: "For her breathing, like his, was loud and shallow." There's the physical reminder of union without a muse. Breathing "loud and shallow" describes too much of my life without writing.

A Brother

When I was young but not a child
I read a story of a sister
and her brother. The two were lovers. Always
when they moved inside each other
they went slowly; if an unexpected twist
lost them in hair in teeth too near
obliteration, at that moment –
about to come – they pulled apart.
Almost too far, they said. Carefully
they moved again: he sang
his traveling songs, she made a story
of his fingers in her hair, their bodies

trembled, the involuntary quiver
easing to a buoyancy
through a long noontime. Outside
a truck's brakes made excruciating noise
and brought them back.

I had forgotten that story, which once shocked
me with what I didn't know, until the night
I dreamed of Paris
(inside me all that beauty)
and alone, my husband gone, a longing
for – I don't know what to call it (is it He?
is it art? is it my heart?) which lay
asleep through movies, car seats, houses –
took hold, stepped out:
                                        water on my body
entered air, my rumpled pin-striped shirt
hung around the doorknob, writings spread
like dunes over both halves of the quilt.
Each thing I loved within my room
stayed visible. And I said
I would make love to my brother
though I have never had a brother.
I could wait. I was a harbor.
I had earth and light to get him to my bed.

   Coming to New York these past three years, working in my
own place, has deepened my relationship with Harold, especially after the trip to Greece with Robert Bly. That changed
us. And though I have felt the comfort of Harold as a brother,
though I love him, he is not my soul's brother. It's the marriage
to myself, my longing for the other I contain, the erotic pleasure of my writing and the world of it, that makes me less crit-
ical of Harold no matter how he breathes. Now I am much less

dependent on his actions for my happiness. The trick is to make room for all I love. Can I?

From Doris Lessing I decide to go to Charlotte Bronte. I've never read *Jane Eyre*. It's so riveting I can hardly think of anything else: Bronte's young girl having fits, her Jane she is transforming through place and time and men and women into the woman who will have a life that fits. It is my story.

The young Jane arouses me to work with a childhood memory of my breathing, the first time I remember holding my breath. Sharon Olds' poems about family, the father in particular, are also close to me these days – I continue to dance with her – so I write:

ON BEING PUSHED WHEN I WAS SEVEN

He threw me in the bay
and I refused to rise.
A friend convinced him
children swim by nature.
So would I. His child,
daughter of the show-off
fighter, I held myself
down, damned
if I'd perform
for any father's friend
who never even glanced
at me. And down there
I took the time to
swear and plan and look
at bubbles coming
from my mouth.
Those men who pulled me out,

they had to pump
like mad. They were the ones
who had to dance.

It has taken me all these years past seven to transform the willful, asthmatic child into the adult that breathes from her solar plexus, the center. Reading and dancing and writing, life is good. When I first worked with Galway on Martha's Vineyard, when I joined the group to go to a disco and found myself dancing and an important poem came, the poem I think of as fueled by my father, I remember how frightened I was by the opening line: "The penis of my father grew." Embarrassed, afraid people would think of incest, I debated whether to keep it. But it's clear; I am the daughter of my mother *and* my father who offer themselves to me as forces from which to create, when I make an effort to be the one who is dancing.

Home

My FOURTH SUBLET WAS MY LAST. As I had guessed, the owners of the sublet on 9th Street didn't live there, and I returned to rent it each September for five years. In the mid-eighties, Harold had a chance to sell his business and decided to do it. In 1988, he joined me in the city, and eventually we bought our own apartment in the Village. Now we are in the city in a new time together.

My work is my center. How I do it is my occupation. From ways learned early on – finding teachers and friends of the heart, making community, paying attention to dreams and to what is in front of my eyes, reading, teaching – I make poems. It is steady practice. In addition to my new family of poets, I have an old family of interesting adults who like what I do. Often I write for them, and for my grandchildren, and for my mother and father and the family no longer here. Often the path to poems and family is travel. The poet William Matthews once told me poets are nomads, which made me feel at home.

Devoted to dreams and travel, in 1994 I flew to Belgium. With the power of the poet I'd become, I used my old dream message, Bruges, the city that mysteriously appeared to me the night my sister-in-law Becky died, to redeem time. Go now, I sensed. It was the week of my sixty-second birthday, May

1994; I didn't know the trip would help me recreate my birth.

I'd been reading in Betty Friedan's book, *The Fountain of Age*, an amazing chapter titled "Going Beyond" about her outward bound experience in her sixties, and I wondered what I wanted to go beyond and realized what I needed to do was go back, catch up. I remembered Bruges, the dream word, the mystery of an unknown, unexplored city. What did it want of me? I decided to fly to Belgium, a country with no identity, on a pilgrimage I thought of as my birthday present.

Before I went to Belgium, Harold and I visited my sister Raina. She and her husband Howard have a winter home in Palm Beach, Florida. Raina and I had planned to drive to Miami to visit, for the first time in seventeen years, the graves of our mother and father. Our husbands were with us. By memory we found our way through the well-kept grass and paths of Lakeside Gardens to the two bronze plates at the foot of their mounds: David M. Stein and to his left Ida Betty Stein, his plate edged in roses, hers in dogwood, his with a star, hers with a candelabrum of lights.

No one else was around; we were quiet, thinking our own thoughts, when Raina said, "I'm telling Mama and Daddy about our good lives, how their struggle produced the happy result of us."

I'd been thinking about my poems which they'd never known. But I said," I forgot we put Mama's middle name on her gravestone. Betty. Remember how she used it to flirt with the maintenance man in her building after Daddy died, when she invited him to dinner in her apartment. She called herself Betty. She gave that name to her unmarried self because she thought it was American and glamorous. How good we knew to celebrate her dreams."

Suddenly, up in a leafy tree, just beyond their graves, we heard a woodpecker, and we laughed. Raina said, "It's Daddy hammering at us for attention." On the opposite, left side of the tree, sitting on bare branches was a gray-breasted bird – a rock dove? – with a dark crown, Mama in her gray club chair, singer refusing to sing while the red-headed woodpecker flitted, displaying himself on the thick, central bark. He allowed us to come close, right to the tree. When we did, the gray bird removed herself to the top of a nearby roofed pavilion. I wanted to go toward her, and as I did, she edged away, always a bit further – "I vant to be alone." The woodpecker stayed where he was and remained quiet as long as someone was watching him. But as soon as we turned to leave, he hammered again. Our husbands were as caught by this scene as we were.

It turned out to be a good prologue to Belgium. My plan was to spend six days there by myself, five of them in Bruges, after which I'd meet Harold. Although Harold had already left his business, and at this point his time was his own, he knew I wanted to go to Belgium alone. From New York he'd fly to Paris to help me celebrate my birthday when I left Bruges.

In Brussels I decided to be slow, to stay close, to eat dinner in my hotel, *le mai diner d'asperges blanche*. All for me, the fresh square of butter, the French roll, the white asparagus. The butter was so deeply sweet my heart skipped. I understand why it's called a spread; I tasted its coming to me through sun and grass and udder, entering me from candlelit china and silver. I was in heaven! And so began the time of babbling to myself.

After such pleasure I was ready to wander out into the balmy wind of the May night, through narrow streets to the center of the city a few blocks away. The Grand Place. There were crowds of people waiting for a light and sound show to begin at ten thirty, and I joined them, marveling at the huge, open space surrounded by beautiful old buildings, thrilled to be an anonymous person in a taupe wool cape about to go forth into my sixty-second year. By the time I got to bed, the excite-

ment of what I was doing had made me manic, and I wanted
to be calm as I'd been at dinner. I looked at maps, tried to plan
my one day in Brussels – what was there in Brussels but the
Mannekin Pis, the city mascot, a statue of a little boy perpetu-
ally peeing?

Finally I fell asleep and dreamt of boring Dalton friends
who came to my birthday with the family. When I woke, I
thought of the poet Robert Creeley with whom I share a birth
date and wondered why I couldn't have dreamt about him.
Maybe the poet was taking her time to arrive.

My afternoon in Brussels I gave to the Musee des Beaux
Arts, the museum which is the title of the W. H. Auden poem I
memorized for Brodsky's class about Breughel's painting of
Icarus drowning in the sea while the world goes on unaware. I
wanted to see that painting. Making my way to it, I stopped to
write in my journal about things that engaged me, as if talking
to a companion.

In a twentieth century room, the entire floor was taken up
by an enormous stone woman stretched across it, face and feet
pointed down; I looked for her name. Niobe. "She's crying
stone tears," that's all I noted. It was getting late and I'd yet to
see the Breughel. When I found the *Fall of Icarus* it was small
and dark, an anti-climax, the poem now forever larger than
the painting that inspired it.

I left the museum to see an American movie, *Ruby in Paradise*, I'd missed back home. In the first shot, Ruby's backing out
of her driveway; we see her license plate and a bumper sticker:
Hamilton County. See Rock City. She's leaving Chattanooga,
Tennessee! Driving into her future! I had no idea. Amazed by
the synchronicity, I felt blessed; I was on my gyroscope.

Next day in Bruges I checked in at the inn I'd chosen from
a guidebook, Die Swaene, charming, situated on a canal, near
the center of town. I was shown my room, a single on the third
floor, the top floor under the eaves. When I went to the dormer

window to open the shutters, there, in my view, on the opposite side of the canal, stretched out over the bank toward the
water was Niobe, a replica of the sculpture I noted the day before when it covered the entire floor of a room at the museum.
I ran downstairs to ask the desk clerk how she happened to be
there – a modern sculpture in this medieval city? He thought
the bank next door placed it.

Niobe. Confronted, I had to pay attention. I remembered
she was a Theban queen punished by the gods, crying eternal
tears for the death of her children. In grief she turned to stone,
and Zeus, taking pity on her, made her into a fountain. Her
tears were filling the canal!

It's you, Mama. I have you in my room's view. In this city
of bridges, this city never destroyed though German bombs lay
eight miles away, in this permanence, I am with you for the five
days before my birth. I am here in a city of beauty and peace
to be delivered. And when at dinner, in the elegant garden of
Die Swaene, I hear a bird singing I laugh, knowing it's you,
Mama. No wonder you're here. *Fineshmecher*, the family called
you, always the romantic, dressing up, loving fine things. Your
beautiful voice singing.

After a walk along the canal in the moonlight, I came back
to my room, to my window and there she was, Niobe, in my
gaze, lit by the moon above the bell tower, and when I fell
asleep, I dreamt of you, Mama, a woman named Moo, holding a blank white, rectangular paper, a tabula rasa I called it,
which I think of as the future. I label it square one.

When it was time to leave Bruges, I felt enlivened, ready to
turn sixty-two with Harold. On the last morning, I went down
to breakfast before catching the train to Paris where Harold
would be waiting. As I walked into the dining room, the in-
evitable walked toward me. "Died. Did you hear? Jackie died."
An American man was reporting the death of Jacqueline
Kennedy Onassis.

I began to cry. The women in the small room, we all looked toward each other as men reached for their newspapers or continued to talk. Staring vacantly, one woman was murmuring in disbelief, "She died."

Who was she to me, to us, to feel so deeply? Years ago when I went to New Orleans with her hairdo, I was thirty. Today Jackie's dead. And I'm going to celebrate my birthday in Paris.

THE FRENCH QUARTER

Through the room women murmur the immensity
Died. I was 30 when,
all night in coach, I sat beside my puzzled husband,
pouffed and ready for –
poetry I called it – the jazzy luxuries of the French Quarter.

30 years later, the train to Paris,
a surge of excitement to see him coming towards the taxi,
his face fresh, child-like
expectation, he wants to show me – after years to say –
look at the rhododendron,

this relais full of flowers and little sitting rooms, our
    room – look
how it faces a fountain –
and we laugh at how few lamps there are, even deluxe,
    his forever
wanting more light,
his fate to be given dark rooms, by now our joke.

Two years after the trip to Bruges, in 1996, Robert Bly chose to edit and publish my manuscript of poems for Blue Sofa Press, a press he'd begun for new writers. On its cover is a painting by Reginald Marsh that hangs in the Hunter Museum of American Art in Chattanooga. It's a subway scene, and I used to visit it, envying the energy and mix of all those people lucky to be living in New York City. When I received permission to use it, I discovered its title is *Subway – 14th Street*. That happens to be my subway stop.

Struggling to come up with the right title for the book, Bly suggested I use *I'll See You Thursday*, my mother's words, the last lines of my poem "Family Jokes": "…If I live and be well I'll see you/ tomorrow; if not, I'll see you Thursday." It is remarkable to me to use what I once thought of as my mother's corny expression for the title of a book. My book! At first I resisted – too prosaic, I said. But Robert knows what he's doing. From a life devoted to poems, he senses the wellspring, my mother's humor, its bravado, as a deep source of the poetry within me. Using my mother's language keeps her alive. I get to hold her close, have her my way. That power writing provides.

It is both heroic and lucky to have given myself what I wanted. Making a writing life in New York City has been like Virginia Woolf's Mrs. Dalloway preparing for her party: leaving her house, going forth (as I left Chattanooga for New York), arranging, planning (the sublets, the workshops) and by evening the guests are at the door, arriving inside (in my case, to share poems, to hear me read, to publish my work). And then, one of Mrs. Dalloway's guests comes to say something like "I'm sorry I'm late; I had to see to the death of a young veteran who committed suicide," and she shouts, silently, "How dare you bring death to my party!"

In the middle of my joy there is a guest at the door who is asking me to make room. This guest crasher (which is the wrong way to name him since he's certainly on the list of arrivals) entered on my sixty-fifth birthday. I mean *knowing* I will die. Knowing, on that birthday, all that remained was about the same number of years I had just given myself in New York.

Suddenly that knowledge walked into my head as real as something in the palm of my hand.

We were in Los Angeles, waiting for the birth, in 1997, of our second grandchild due on the day of my sixty-fifth birthday. When May twenty-first came, I, who had planned each birthday since I was fifty to be what I wanted or sensed the year ahead would want to bring me, decided to let be, just let the day come, no calling of poet-friends in the area to join me, no excursions to the island of Catalina or the Shangri-La of Ojai, just a nice dinner, a pretty table surrounded by my husband and daughter Karen and her husband Syud and Benjamin, our first grandson, just that.

And then the revelation, the fact that it had been sixteen years since I arrived in New York to write poetry; sixteen years of a true life, my heart's life, had passed. Because I was so conscious of the years, never taking them for granted, they felt solid enough to hold. I *realized* them, and I realized I had only one more handful to go; fifteen years would bring me to eighty. I couldn't get over such a fact.

Only one more go round – and only if I'm lucky. So my job became getting used to it. Finding what the good way out would be. How to make the reality of death taste right. It seemed a sour soup I couldn't mix the ingredients for.

How dare you bring death to my party? I couldn't stop saying it. When I arranged to give my New York City reading in 1997 for my book of poems, *I'll See You Thursday*, I chose a bookstore next to NYU buildings, Posman's, two blocks from where I'd leased my fourth sublet. It was fairly new to the neighborhood. I didn't want a Barnes and Noble (though there is a grand-looking one at Union Square, and my book has the subway at Union Square on its cover). I wanted an independent bookstore with personal warmth. Instead of reading alone, I decided to ask Frannie, whom I'd met when we first worked with Galway Kinnell and Sharon Olds on Martha's Vineyard, to read with me. She lives out on the end of Long Island, and her first book, *The Widow's Quilt*, was published around the same time as mine. The date was set for a Sunday afternoon in March.

On the morning of the reading the call came. Frannie's ninety-year-old mother had died. She'd been ill. When the phone rang I knew what I was about to hear, that death was coming to my party. And because Frannie decided to go ahead with the reading, although I suggested she might not want to, and I told her I could certainly go on alone, because I couldn't scream *don't*, except silently, Death became the event.

I'd never heard her give a better reading. She introduced a guest in the audience who was covering the Vietnam War with her husband when he died and then she told of her mother's death that morning. I read after her, confused, feeling cheated.

With husbands and friends we went out for dinner; I couldn't choose my place at the table. Instead I decided to go to the bathroom first, and when I returned, Frannie's friend was sitting in the center seat across from her, Goldilocks sitting in my chair. Again I left for the bathroom. Back and forth.

After that day I could hardly be with Frannie. I made the appropriate condolence call, but later I began to get headaches when I was with her. She is my close friend. I had to say something that was hardly rational, something out of proportion. I had to confess my resentment, and trust she would remain my friend. The alternative seemed wrong, to stay away and bury our friendship. So my crass confession raised itself beside the loss of her mother; I made myself say my words of bitterness; she let herself hear. Of course, days had to pass, but our friendship endured.

From the start, from the death of my sister before I was born, death has mixed itself with my life. My job up to now may have been to make sure they stayed apart. But it's no longer

possible, and I want to learn to open the door to the guest I've
refused admission to the party. *Rage, rage against the dying of
the light* sang Dylan Thomas's passion, but it is not what I want
in my mouth. The oil is beginning to ask for the vinegar. If I can
learn to dress this salad just right, I'll toss it as I did when I
came to New York, singing *Gloria*.

It's twenty years past my sublets; Harold and I have just come
from an evening with a group of friends from Poets House, a
new poetry library on whose board of directors I've come to
serve. Also with us were writer friends we met through Robert
Bly. The occasion was a Lincoln Center Festival production of
the *Edda*, Icelandic tales recited to music. Those stories begin
when the world is new, in tranquility; then, with the advent of
people, they become tales of struggle, greed, love, wars, revenge, hacking of bodies, fire, more revenge until everyone is
destroyed, and there is nothing but quiet, out of which green
springs again. That's where the performance ends. I sat there
thinking these might be ancient tales but here we are in the
summer of 2001 with wars brewing all over the world, with
nuclear bombs and their power set to destroy us by fire.

After Harold sold his business, and came to the city, he
began in 1990 to devote himself to organizations that work for
peace in the Middle East where the *Edda* tales indeed feel current. Good friends in Israel had sent us writings about the in-
tifada, uprisings in the occupied territories, and some terrible
things Jews were doing in response to it. Harold insisted Jewish people wouldn't engage in such cruelties to others, so our
friends, who are educators as well as political activists working
to end the occupation, responded, "Come to Israel for just one
week; then we'll talk." And in that winter of 1990 we went.
Our friends set up what they called a crash course; each day we
visited important Israeli and Palestinian leaders, Knesset members, journalists, professors. We were in Gaza the day a young

boy throwing stones was killed by soldiers. By the end of that week Harold was radicalized, and his work has become an attempt to create, in the United States, awareness of the Middle East struggle.

As we listened to the *Edda* with its haunting reminder of current violence, I thought if the world were to end at this moment, my poet friends next to me, I wouldn't be terrified. That was my feeling.

I want to spit three times, or some such, to ward off the jinx of such a thought – words, even said to oneself, have mysterious power – but what I mean to convey is this knowledge of serenity. I have found my way to my place, to my story, the once upon a time that ends in my soul's happily ever after.

Recently I left the apartment, wearing sandals, a shiny pink, too-tight T-shirt and dirty, light blue jeans, and headed for a neighborhood breakfast meeting with a friend from Poets House. I'd overslept and had to hurry.

Walking along Lafayette Street to the Noho Star, I slowed down, smiling because the Village was so fresh in early morning. I'm hardly ever out at nine a.m. The furniture stores that line Lafayette were closed. Their fifties Danish designs, which filled my modest house in Chattanooga, sat expensively in the windows. I passed the Public Theatre; it always tugs at my heart with memories of its founder, Joseph Papp. Down South, in a game called Facts in Five, I would list Papp under P when theatre was the category, and my brother-in-law, who'd never heard of Papp, swore I cheated. "C'mon, you're pulling him out of your New York hat so you think we have to believe you." He knew New York was where I always lived. I'd try to convince by details: the son of Jewish immigrants who loves Shakespeare, who produces the plays in Central Park and sees that they're free for people to enjoy every summer. It was my usual spiel about greatness in New York. Now Papp is gone, but his gift to the city remains, the Public Theatre *in my neighborhood* on my way to talk about poems.

My friend was waiting. I helped her with a sonnet sequence she was creating to explore her love of Italy, her birthplace. She helped me with a poem that wanted to speak of last things, "The Late Lover."

"What you've done in the first two stanzas is strong," she said, referring to the daughter watching her mother's old age flirtations, "but as soon as you say you're scared, knowing you save the best for last, and we wait for what you're about to do, the poem gets obscure. Exactly what is it you wish for your old age here?"

Oh boy, I had to figure what desire I was camouflaging with allusions to John Berryman's Mr. Bones whom I suddenly addressed in my poem: "Tell me you want me bad. Bad enough to do/ an old woman's/ dirty work. Shine so bright there is no dirty work."

My friend laughed, "Sounds like a joyous request for a physical life." She suggested I express it without using Berryman, or make the connection clearer.

I squirmed, confessing as I yanked at my shirt, "You've given me insight into stuff I probably wanted to avoid."

We hugged goodbye in front of the number 6 subway line on the corner of Bleecker. I thought how easy it would be to hop on an uptown train and in no time be at Lord & Taylor's trying on bathing suits for a trip I was about to take with Harold. My old suit was faded and stretched; I never find time to shop, so while I was out, the subway at my feet, I could do it. And I did.

In my junky clothes I was on Fifth Avenue, entering a department store, taking the up escalator. Shades of my mother, the world's indefatigable shopper. Only she would be wearing necklace and earrings.

In August, all that remained were ugly swim suits. I was surrounded by racks and racks of fall skirts and sweaters and suits and coats. *Suffocated* is the word that came over me, and the fact that it was a word and not my life saved me, distancing me from distress, the way I'm not my mother who had no Women's Movement but mostly shopping and cooking and card games to give her activity and options.

I knew the New York Public Library was just two blocks north where *Such Friends*, an exhibit of Yeats' poems and memorabilia, waited to be seen. I'd been planning to go. Yes, even for a little while, I'd take myself there, knowing the next week I could return with more time.

There he is. William Butler Yeats struggling with Maud Gonne again. I'm thunder-struck by Gonne's telling Yeats she conceived her daughter in the memorial room of her dead son. Her courage and passion urge me to mine; once more I accept how death and birth came together and created me. I stop to read Crazy Jane's words: "But Love has pitched his mansion in/ The place of excrement;/ For nothing can be sole or whole/ That has not been rent."

When I left the apartment in the morning, I said I'd be back in a few hours and here it is, late afternoon. Walking toward the subway at Grand Central Station, I think about Harold and me going down the subway stairs after buying our new apartment, how we left the lawyer's office with its talk of hundreds of thousands of dollars and took a subway back to the sublet. What was my joy? That an apartment in a New York City skyscraper was to be mine, and so were the subways?

That was my mother's joke. She loved the sign in the subway car with its cockamamie claim: *Don't spit. The subways are yours.* Remembering, I have to laugh. The subways are mine.

About the Author

Myra Shapiro, born in the Bronx, returned to New York after forty-five years in Georgia and Tennessee where she married, raised two daughters, and worked as a librarian and teacher of English. She received her M.F.A. from Vermont College in 1993. Her poems have appeared in *Calyx*, *Harvard Review*, *Hunger Mountain*, *Ploughshares*, and *Rattapallax* among other periodicals and in numerous anthologies, most recently *Family Reunion: Poems about Parenting Grown Children* and the *Best American Poetry, 1999* and *2003*. She received the Dylan Thomas Poetry Award from the New School and was the finalist in 2005 for the Robert H. Winner Memorial Award from the Poetry Society of America. She has enjoyed residencies at the MacDowell Colony, Hedgebrook, and the Banff Arts Centre. She serves on the board of directors of Poets House, is a member of PEN, and teaches poetry workshops for the International Women's Writing Guild. Her book of poems, *I'll See You Thursday*, was published in 1996 by Blue Sofa Press.

Order Form

Chicory Blue Press, Inc.
795 East Street North
Goshen, CT 06756
860/491-2271
860/491-8619 (fax)
sondraz@optonline.net
www.chicorybluepress.com

Please send me the following books:

_____ copies of *Four Sublets: Becoming a Poet in New York* at $18.00

_____ copies of *What if your mother* at $15.00

_____ copies of *The* Love *Word* at $18.00

_____ copies of *Resistance* at $16.00

_____ copies of *Family Reunion* at $18.00

_____ copies of *The Crimson Edge* at $17.95

_____ copies of *A Wider Giving* at $14.95

Name _____

Address_____

_____

_____

Connecticut residents: Please add sales tax.

Shipping: Add $4.00 for the first book and $1.50 for each additional book.